Herbs

By the Editors of *Sunset Books* and *Sunset Magazine*

LANE PUBLISHING CO.
MENLO PARK, CALIFORNIA

Foreword

The particular fascination of herbs, with their fragrances, flavors, beauty, and value, is attested to by the fact that people have been growing and using them for thousands of years. In this book we have tried to present many of the attractions of herbs, while at the same time keeping uppermost the how-to's of growing them. Staff researcher-writer Richard Osborne produced the basic manuscript, with consultation and help from Ed Carman, nurseryman; Mrs. Ralph Cross; Mrs. Roxana Ferris, botanist; Mrs. Chas. L. Gannaway; Frank Prouty, nurseryman; Wayne Roderick, horticulturist; Mrs. Fitzhugh Rollins; and Mrs. Constance Saroyan.

Supervising Editor: Philip Edinger

Design: Lawrence A. Laukhuf

Illustrations: E. D. Bills

Front cover: Wooden planter filled with silver thyme, sage, marjoram, chives, and spearmint with dittany of Crete in clay container. Photograph by Ells Marugg.
Design consultant: John Flack.

Sunset Books
Editor, David E. Clark
Managing Editor, Elizabeth L. Hogan

Sixteenth printing January 1988

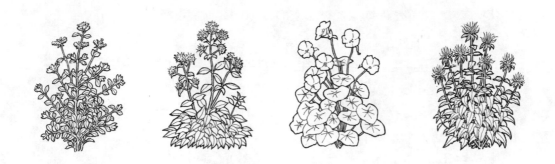

Contents

SPRINGTIME GARDEN ACTIVITIES *are shown in this 16th century engraving. Workers in the foreground prepare beds for herb planting while others sow seeds and set out new plants.*

The Lore and Lure of Herbs

T HE IMPORTANCE OF HERBS dates back thousands of years. They have been used in cooking and medicine, as fragrances, and for ornament. Today, the popularity of these plants can be attributed to their numerous practical uses, which gives them an appeal to gardeners and non-gardeners alike.

• Cooks enjoy a favorite herb or two growing near the kitchen door or window where they are handy for picking and using to season foods.

• Lovers of fragrances will find in herbs a wealth of pleasing aromas that can be used in making potpourris, sachets, and bouquets.

• The flowers of herbs such as yarrows, violets, and the old roses lend color to the garden and to cut arrangements; others such as borage and dittany have small blossoms with fascinatingly delicate features.

• In the landscape, herbs serve as fillers between other plants, as background or low foreground plants, as ground covers, and as hedges. Many of them have interesting textures or gray foliage that provide garden contrasts and highlights; others will grow in locations where more sensitive plants would die.

• In containers, herbs make attractive and fragrant ornamentals for the patio, kitchen, and living room.

• Most of the herbs have a history of medicinal uses, and some are still used as health foods, nutritional supplements, and home remedies for minor ailments.

• Folklore enthusiasts will be intrigued by the myths, history, and early uses of herbs.

Besides these numerous appeals and uses, herbs are easy to grow and require only a small amount of care and attention. You can grow only one or two kinds without any more commitment to them than an occasional watering and trimming. If you have no outdoor garden space you still can grow herbs, as most of them will be happy indoors.

As you grow herbs and become more interested in them, there is no limit to the possible depth of your involvement with these plants. You might discover a particular favorite herb and begin a collection of all its species or varieties. Or, you might decide you'd like to grow the herbs used by a particular culture such as an American Indian tribe that once lived in your area; this adds a new dimension to collecting native plants. For historical appeal, you might want a garden containing herbs mentioned in the Bible or those that Shakespeare referred to in his plays. More exotic would be a collection of Oriental, African, or South American herbs. Still another possibility—with almost endless variations—is a garden of culinary, medicinal, or perfumery herbs, both those still used for these purposes and others no longer employed by modern cultures.

However you grow herbs and whatever is your interest in them, they will open a marvelous world of beauty, flavor, fragrance, and folklore for you to explore.

WHAT IS AN HERB?

There are three generally accepted definitions of an herb. Botanically, herbs are non-woody annual, biennial, and perennial plants that die back each year after blossoming. Another definition describes them as any of the herbaceous plants valued for their flavor, fragrance, or medicinal properties. The third is actually not a definition but a distinction between the culinary herbs and spices.

The botanical definition includes many plants that we ordinarily think of as weeds (and even eliminate from the garden when they appear) and therefore never cultivate as we do marjoram or sage. Many vegetables and ornamental garden plants also fit this description, but they are not usually thought of as herbs. Excluded by the definition are a number of shrubby and woody plants such as laurel and rosemary, which for centuries have been two of the most distinguished herbs.

More flexible is the second definition which singles out herbs as being useful as flavoring, scents, or medicine. But, because our uses of various plants change as our needs do, a list of plants that could be considered useful will differ from culture to culture and from century to century. Also, this definition does not distinguish fragrant flowers such as gardenias from the fragrant herbs such as lavender and germander.

In cooking, a distinction is made between spices and herbs. Spices usually are considered to be derived from the roots, bark, fruit, or berries of perennial plants such as cinnamon, ginger, nutmeg, and pepper; herbs are the leaves only of low growing shrubs and herbaceous plants such as basil, rosemary, and thyme. There are several plants, however—such as some of the roses—which are included in herb listings even though their fruit (rose hips) is used.

Because of these complications in defining herbs, it is perhaps easier to understand their nature through the ways they have been used and thought of in the past.

HERBS IN LITERATURE AND LEGEND

The earliest sources of herb lore and usage are ancient Greek and Roman poetry and myths and the Bible. These references provide us with many of the popular beliefs and conceptions of plants in these times.

Some herbs such as dittany of Crete and rue were supposed to have been given by the gods to mankind or to a hero to help them cure sickness and wounds or to avert disaster. Other herbs were thought to be divine because, as described in the myths of Apollo and Daphne (page 75) and that of Pluto and Menthe (page 69) they were created by a metamorphosis of a man or god into a plant.

One of the fascinating things about these myths is the close tie between the origin of an herb and the way it was used. Because Aeneas was believed to have used dittany to heal the wounds of his soldiers, it was said that animals wounded by hunters ate the leaves to remove the spear or arrow that had struck them and to heal the wound.

If a god was somehow associated with a particular herb, perhaps because he gave it to a hero or had been changed into it through a metamorphosis, it was usually thought to be favored by him and therefore used to decorate his temple and to honor him in ceremonies.

Another ancient use of herbs was in religious rituals and sacred offerings to the gods. The fragrant herbs were burned as incense in belief that their sweet smelling smoke would rise into the heavens and please the gods. For the same purpose, they were placed on sacred animals that were burned in sacrifices.

The Bible has several references to herbs and their uses. One of these suggests that herbs were used as payment for taxes and tithes.

> Woe unto you, scribes and Pharisees, hypocrites! for ye pay tithe of mint and anise and cumin and have omitted the weightier matters of the law, judgment, mercy, and faith; these ye ought to have done and not to leave the other undone.

Some herbs such as rosemary and angelica were considered holy because a Saint or Apostle was said to have blessed them, performed a miracle with them, or used them in some other special way.

There are also references to myrrh, calamus, and other fragrant herbs being burned as incense and added to sacred oils for anointing priests. Pungent herbs such as hyssop were used to cleanse the body and soul, purifying them of disease and sin. Hyssop was also used to protect the houses of good men from plagues, which were thought to be sent as a punishment for wickedness. A number of the bitter herbs were eaten during Passover.

The first formal plant studies were made by ancient Greek and Roman scholars. Since most plants were first valued because they could be used to fulfill a need, these studies focused mainly upon the *uses* of plants rather than on their botanical differences.

Theophrastus of Eresus (370 B.C.), a Grecian scholar who studied under both Plato and Aristotle, was perhaps the greatest and most influential of the early writers about plants. His *Historia Plantarum* is the earliest botanical work known and was the greatest single influence on the study of plants for the next 1,800 years. The book describes a great number of plants, tells where they grew, and what they look like and were used for. He also classified plants into four groups: trees, shrubs, half-shrubs, and herbs—a system that often still is used today. His studies investigate seed germination, perfumes, and medi-

ANCIENT Greece and Rome used dittany of Crete as a cure for wounds. Today it is an excellent ornamental.

CALIFORNIA BAY (Umbellularia californica) has leaves with a flavor similar to sweet bay (Laurus nobilis).

cal usage. These first hand observations have been so highly regarded as foundational for modern plant study that Theophrastus is considered the "Father of Modern Botany."

Other great writers during these periods are Claudius Galen (130-200 A.D.), and Caius Plinius Secundus, born in 23 A.D., who held the distinction of having acquired the total sum of knowledge of his time. In his *Natural History*, Pliny described individual plants, their most pertinent distinctions and uses, the diseases of plants, and other information about their growth and habits that he had accumulated from his reading and observations.

THE HERBALISTS AND HERBAL MEDICINE

After Galen, the study of plants was continued mostly by monks. A number of monastaries cultivated what were known as "physic" gardens which consisted of medical herbs and were often opened to the public.

Some rulers, notably Charlemagne, encouraged botanical study by sponsoring gardens in which plants from different parts of the country could be grown and studied. Secular interest in herbs and other plants reached a height during the 15th through 17th centuries and took several forms including written works, popular usage, and the development of ornamental gardens.

The most popular and far reaching form of herb study was a type of book known as the herbal. These books combined botanical information with herbal remedies, cooking recipes, and general household herb uses. Typically, an herbal would contain descriptions of every useful plant known to the writer, popular beliefs about where to grow them, their compatibility with one another, and any peculiarities of use, harvesting, and propagation. Along with the author's personal observation, information in the medieval herbals was gathered from writings of other herbalists, ancient writers, hearsay, and superstition. Among the best are Gerard's *Herball or General Historie of Plants*, and the works of John Parkinson. Other herbals such as Culpepper's *Complete Herbal* are fascinating to read, but much of their information is questionable or highly impractical.

In their study of herbal medicine, the herbalists had several interesting approaches. One of the most intriguing was known as the "Doctrine of Signatures." In this school of thought each plant was named after and used to cure a part of the body or a disease whose appearance it most resembled. The leaves of lungwort (*Pulmonaria*), for example, were taken to resemble diseased lungs, and hence they were thought to cure chest ailments, the lungs, and breathing difficulties. Eyebright has flowers that look like bloodshot eyes, and they were used to treat cataracts and blindness. In this manner arose an interesting array of plant names and fantastic cures for almost every disease and part of the body. When we read of all the illness that plants with such names as "allheal" and "selfheal" were supposed to cure, it is a mystery how someone's death was accounted for when these plants were available.

Another, perhaps more esoteric, approach to herbal medicine was through astrology. Each herb was associated with one of the 7 planets known at the time and with one of the 12 signs of the zodiac whose characteristics it most resembled. Similarly, the parts of the body were given astrological significance. Curing an illness was then a matter of using the herb whose planet and sign were sympathetic to or strengthening to the part of the body that was afflicted.

Besides these pseudoscientific studies of herbal medicine, both wild and cultivated herbs were also used in folk remedies that had been passed down for centuries from generation to generation.

Though most of these early herbal remedies have highly exaggerated curative powers that were often based purely on superstition, some actually may have had a degree of effectiveness. A number of herbs have high concentra-

tions of vitamins: Spearmint and catnip, for example, are rich in vitamin C. If the illnesses they were used to treat were caused by simple vitamin deficiencies, eating quantities of an herb would have had the beneficial effect of replenishing the shortage.

Derivatives from herbs such as foxglove and opium poppy are still used as drugs to treat some of the same ailments for which the herbalists used them. Some of the old folk remedies such as horehound for a cough and catnip tea for sleeplessness still are used occasionally today.

FRAGRANCES, COOKING, ORNAMENT

In addition to their widespread employment as medicines, herbs were used for their fragrances, as disinfectants, in cooking, and for decoration.

In medieval times when fresh air was considered unhealthy, there was a great need for both air fresheners and sweet fragrances. Herbs provided these in several ways. Nosegays, consisting of fragrant herb leaves wrapped in small pieces of cloth, could be carried with a person and sniffed whenever a breath of refreshing fragrance was

LUNGWORT was one of the many medieval medicinal herbs. The leaves are light green mottled with white.

SOFT AND FRAGRANT is this garden bench planted with thyme. A 3-inch layer of soil provides for the roots.

desired. It was thought that different aromas each had a special effect on a person. Nosegays of thyme leaves were thought to refresh a tired person; sweetbriar was believed to make one cheerful; and others made from different combinations of herbs would refresh the memory or ease tension.

Pomander balls were another aromatic. These were apples or oranges filled with cloves and other herbs and spices. They could be hung indoors in a room to deodorize the air or be worn on a belt or necklace.

Rooms of a house were also perfumed by fragrant herbs such as marjoram, rosemary, and thyme placed or "strewn" on the floors for occasions such as weddings, feasts, and coronations. When walked upon, their fragrances were released to sweeten the air.

The aroma of herbs such as hyssop and rue were thought to be disinfectant and they were strewn on the floors of jails to control diseases that often infested them. Bunches of these herbs were also placed on the judge's bench in courtrooms to protect the judges from diseases carried by the prisoners.

Herbs were then, as now, used as foods and seasonings. However, there were a number of differences from contemporary cookery. From old recipes and cookbooks it appears that foods were generally more highly seasoned than they are today. Herbs such as hyssop, whose flavor is unpalatable to many modern tastes, were used to season a number of foods. Rather than being used to enhance the natural flavor of food, herbs were frequently used to preserve meat from spoiling, or to disguise or overpower the taste and smell of decay. Salads of the past were also quite different, often containing over 30 different kinds of leaves, herbs, roots, seeds, and vegetables.

Vegetables as we know and eat them did not become a substantial part of a meal until the 16th and 17th centuries. Until then, they were eaten mainly for their health-giving qualities. Thus, many of the plants that we now include in our regular diet as vegetables were then considered herbs.

Early gardens grown by commoners and cooks were designed mostly for utility rather than pleasure, and they contained only the plants that were to be used in the household. Other gardens were grown by early botanists and monks so that plants could be studied more conveniently than if they were in the fields and woods.

As members of the wealthier classes in the Middle Ages and Renaissance found more time for pleasure, they began to include gardening and gardens as one of their recreations and developed gardens in which leisure time could be spent enjoying the beauty of the plants. Monks, housewives, cooks, and apothecaries continued to grow their plants for use, but courts and rich landowners would also maintain ornamental gardens as a necessary luxury, like a ballroom or stable of fine horses, befitting their station in life. These early pleasure gardens included the useful cooking and medicinal plants, but gradually became refined to only the more decorative kinds.

Walls of brick or stone, or high hedges, usually enclosed the gardens, and the plants inside grew in orderly and geometrically shaped beds separated by garden paths that often were covered with chamomile or sweet woodruff. Some gardens had earthen benches along their walls on which were planted creeping thyme that would release a pleasant fragrance when someone sat on them. A fountain, bird bath, or sundial sometimes formed a central figure.

Knot gardens, which reached the height of their vogue during the Renaissance, were intricate, low plantings of herbs that interlaced one another and resembled a knotted rope.

Another type of popular garden was the "sundial garden." It consisted of plants whose flowers opened and closed at different times of the day planted in a circular bed in the form of a clock or sundial.

Victorian herb gardens were very geometric, with the plants growing in square or triangular beds. Straight paths between them increased the sense of structured patterns.

TRADITIONAL formal herb garden includes symmetrical planting beds, paths bordered with boxwood, and birdbath.

FOXGLOVE, *once a medicinal herb, is a source of digitalis. Today it is used as a garden ornamental.*

The modern word *herb* is derived from the Latin *herba*—which means grass. Until the 16th century the English version was spelled *erb*, after the Old French spelling *erbe*, and was pronounced as it was spelled. When the "h" was added in the 1500's, the pronunciation remained the same until the 19th century when the sounding of the formerly silent letter became popular in England. Now, both the erb and herb pronunciations are considered correct, and both versions have strong advocates.

In the advance of modern science and medicine, there has been a decline in the home use of plants as medicines, disinfectants, and food preservatives. Some former herbs—deprived of their medieval usefulness—have become thought of as weeds, or are now incorporated into our regular diet as vegetables. Others that no longer have their medicinal value gained a new status as flowers and decorative garden plants.

Some plants, however, have retained their everyday uses and/or still are remembered and valued for their historical usage: These are the plants most commonly considered to be modern herbs.

ROSE GERANIUM *is one of the many scented pelargoniums that have a fruity fragrance. In mild climates they are all-year garden ornamentals; in areas where winters are severe they can be brought indoors in containers.*

The most universally recognized of these contemporary uses is in seasoning foods. Even if we don't add herbs to foods ourselves, they often are added to canned and frozen foods, or they are major ingredients of prepared sauces and dressings.

Fragrant herbs also have maintained their usefulness into modern times. Although potpourris and strewing herbs are no longer used to disinfect the air, herbs are still pleasant reminders of the garden and are frequently used in fresh and dried flower arrangements. Many are ingredients of fine commercial perfumes.

Most of the early medicinal herbs are no longer used in home remedies but are often included in the herb garden because of their historical background or for their attractiveness in plantings with other herbs.

Many of the modern herbs now cultivated in the United States and Europe are from the Mediterranean countries. From there they were spread to the rest of Western Europe by the Romans, early traders, and the Crusaders; they immigrated to America with the first settlers who brought with them seeds of the plants they had known in their homelands. A few herbs such as nasturtiums are native to South and Central America and were taken to North America and Europe by the early Spanish explorers.

Most of these herbs fall into three major families. The mint family (Labiatae) includes basil, lavender, marjoram, the mints, rosemary, sage, savory, and thyme. The family Compositae (which also includes ornamental daisies) consists of the artemisias, chamomile, tansy, and yarrows. Members of the Umbelliferae, or carrot family, are anise, angelica, caraway, chervil, sweet cicely, coriander, dill, fennel, lovage, and parsley; they are characterized by finely cut and divided foliage and by their tap roots.

There are, of course, plants native to various parts of the world which are used locally as herbs by the people living in those areas. Most of the American Indian tribes had uses for native plants such as slippery elm, sassafras, yerba buena, and chaparral, and many of them were adopted by settlers who moved into tribal territories. Almost entirely different herbs than those which we commonly use from the Mediterranean areas are found in the Orient, Africa, and South America.

In this book we have included the herbs most commonly grown in the United States today. All of them have everyday uses as seasonings, in fragrant preparations, or in the landscape. They are listed, illustrated, and described—along with cooking tips and other uses—on pages 56-79. Recipes for various herbal preparations such as potpourris, teas, jellies, and vinegars are given on pages 50-55. A number of ideas for growing herbs in the landscape, containers, and indoors are described and pictured on pages 13-37.

FLAT FLOWER CLUSTERS identify a typical member of the Umbelliferae family which contains many popular herbs.

SQUARE STEMS and heavily veined leaves of this spearmint sprig are typical of members of the Labiatae family.

BORDERED WITH SANTOLINAS (gray santolina, S. chamaecyparissus on the left, S. virens on right) this garden path leads to a bird bath surrounded by southernwood which has gray foliage in overlapping layers.

Where to Grow the Versatile Herbs

THERE ARE MANY different kinds of herbs and your first step in planning a garden is to choose the ones you want to grow. If you are new to herb gardening you will probably want to start with those that you can have the most fun using. Culinary and fragrant herbs can be used to make teas, jellies, herbed butters and breads, and preparations such as potpourris and sachets. Herbs such as the santolinas and artemisias are most useful as a landscape feature; others are grown mainly for their exotic appeal and interesting histories. A number of different culinary, fragrant, and ornamental herbs are described on pages 56-79.

Gardeners in many areas of the West and Southwest (and, generally, where winter temperatures never drop below 0°) have the opportunity to use many of the shrubby Mediterranean herbs as basic landscape items. The rosemaries, lavenders, and marjoram, for example, will grow larger and more attractive each year, planted outside.

There is no set way or place to grow your herbs. They can be raised like vegetables in rows or plots, neatly staked off and labeled. You can integrate them into the landscape as ground covers, edgings, or companion plants with other ornamentals. (See pages 18-29.) Or, more casual plantings can grow in corners of the garden or small sections of a border. You also can grow herbs in containers both outside and indoors. (See pages 30-37 for indoor and container culture.) If you are more ambitious and want to be traditional, you can plan the kind of formal herb garden which originated in the Middle Ages.

It is best to keep those herbs that require different amounts of water (such as the mints and thyme) at separate ends of the bed. Some herbs do not require as much sun as the others and can be planted near taller kinds that will filter direct sunlight before it reaches them. Or, you can locate the bed where one section will receive fewer hours of sunlight each day than the rest of the bed. Aggressive or persistent herbs such as lemon balm, the mints, and sweet woodruff, should not be positioned where they can crowd out the others. Plant them in a separate bed or contain their roots with divider boards sunk into the ground around them and keep the runners that spread along the ground cut back.

Most perennial and annual herbs can be started from seeds in the fall or spring (pages 38-42), but if you just want to grow a few plants it is often easier to buy them from a nursery. As perennials grow larger, you can increase your stock by division, stem cuttings, or layering as described on pages 43-45. A small planting of annual herbs should produce enough seeds to give you a greater number of plants the following year.

If you intend to sow seeds of slow germinating perennial herbs in the fall followed by seeds of annual herbs in the spring, plan spacing for the whole garden in the fall and carefully recultivate the bed in the spring so you don't disturb the germinating perennials. An alternative is to sow the perennial seeds elsewhere in the fall, and then in the spring transplant the seedlings into a freshly prepared bed where you can also sow annual seeds.

CULINARY PLANTINGS of several useful herbs just outside the kitchen door are convenient for the cook.

CONCRETE BLOCKS can be buried on their sides to make neat planters for a number of different culinary herbs.

CULINARY HERB PLANTINGS

Here is a list of common culinary and fragrant herbs whose leaves are frequently used: basil, borage, burnet, chervil, chives, dill, fennel, garlic, lemon balm, lemon verbena, marjoram, mint, oregano, parsley, rose geranium, sage, summer and winter savory, tarragon, and thyme. A few herbs whose seeds are often used in cooking are anise, caraway, dill, and coriander.

Rather than start with all of these, you may prefer to try just a few of the ones that you would normally buy at the store such as basil, chives, marjoram, mint, rosemary, tarragon, and thyme. Or, you may want to browse through the herbal on pages 56-79 and choose the ones that sound most interesting to you.

The number of plants of each herb you grow will depend on the amount of garden or container space you have and the ways you intend to use their leaves, flowers, and seeds. Some of the more popular culinary herbs such as basil, chives, marjoram, mint, rosemary, and thyme can be used in many different foods and recipes. All of them except basil and parsley are perennial and can grow large enough in the garden in warm winter climates that 2 or 3 plants of each should provide enough leaves for use throughout the year. In colder regions where perennials die back in the winter, you probably will want a few more plants to provide leaves to dry for winter use in addition to those plants which will furnish fresh leaves during the summer. You also might want one or two plants to grow in containers indoors during the winter.

The annual herbs will die after flowering, and unless you plan to raise a crop indoors in the winter, your supply for the year must be grown during the summer. If you intend to cure a crop of leaves and also want some to use fresh, plan to grow about 10-12 plants of each. Otherwise, about 4-6 plants should produce enough leaves for summer use.

A large number of culinary herbs are easiest to raise and care for when they are planted in rows in a single, well-prepared bed. The size of the plot depends entirely on the space you have available and how many plants you intend to grow. Spacing requirements for many of the herbs are given in their description in the herbal on pages 56-79 and can usually be found on seed packages. The ideal location for a garden of this sort is a sunny spot that will receive 6-8 hours of full sun each day. The soil's pH should be neutral or slightly alkaline for most of the herbs, and above all it should be well drained. Directions for preparing the bed and sowing the seeds are given on pages 38-42.

There are, of course, many other ways to grow culinary herbs. Small plantings can be raised in a flower border, out-of-the-way corner of the yard, or any convenient location where they will receive adequate sunlight.

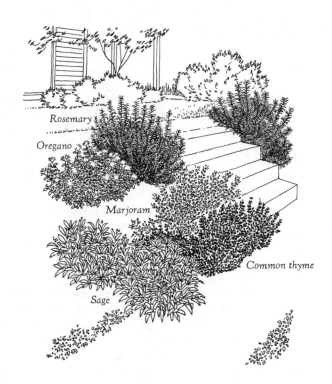

SUN-LOVING HERBS *line these steps leading to a back porch. The slope provides for good drainage.*

ALONG A PATH *herbs provide an interesting border of various textures and tones of green and gray.*

THREE CULINARY HERBS—*chives, parsley, and mint—grow happily in this planter just outside the kitchen door. The mint is planted in a pail plunged into the box to keep its roots from spreading.*

🌿 FORMAL GARDENS

Formal herb gardens have taken many forms over the centuries. Knot gardens (page 9) are one of the most traditional. Another form is the "sundial" garden of flowers that open at different times of the day.

Designing and maintaining a formal herb garden requires more time and work (especially in year-round gardening areas) than less formal plantings, but the reward can be a uniquely peaceful garden with an atmosphere of serene beauty.

The first step in planning a formal herb garden is to decide its size and location. The site must receive enough sunlight for the herbs to thrive. The garden can be as small or large as you want it to be or have room for. Perhaps you have a sunny utility area between the side of the house and a fence that is too narrow or small for other plants. A place in the yard that you have not landscaped because no one spends enough time there could make a peaceful retreat for meditation. Or, you might simply use a corner in the yard formed by two intersecting fences. Wherever you think about placing the garden, remember that it does not have to be square or rectangular, though most are symmetrical in layout.

After deciding a place for the formal herb garden, decide which herbs you want to use. Keeping the size and shape of the garden in mind, plan the layout of the planting beds and walks.

There are limitless designs for formal herb gardens. The planting beds can be geometrically shaped like triangles, rectangles, or semicircles, with one or two herbs planted in each and paths separating them. Or, you can plant a number of different herbs in each bed to emphasize their differences in texture and growth patterns. For example, taller herbs could grow at the back of the plots with lower ones in the front. Herbs with varying shades and tones of gray and green offer interesting contrasts and harmonies. You could design an Elizabethan knot garden with line-like plantings of low growing herbs interweaving one another in patterns emphasized by different tones and textures of foliage. Even small areas can feature herbs growing in a formal plan as on either side of a path which leads to a piece of garden sculpture or encircles a bird bath.

After planning the design of your garden, prepare the planting beds as described on pages 39-40. To make the garden easier to maintain and to help keep the herbs growing neatly, sink divider boards into the ground to define the areas in which each herb or group of herbs will grow. These retainers will provide guides for planting and

FORMAL HERB GARDEN features pathways planted with cotula and a sundial surrounded by lemon geranium. Borders consist of santolina, germander, hyssop, marjoram, dwarf myrtle, and red yarrow.

to some degree keep the roots and runners of the herbs within their bounds.

Next, establish the garden's paths so that you will have a convenient place to stand while planting the herbs. Flagstone or brick (especially used brick) lend an antique appearance to a formal herb garden, enhancing its "traditional" quality.

In many herb gardens paths are covered with one of the fragrant ground cover herbs (see pages 24-26). If you decide to plant one of these herbs on the paths, cultivate the ground where the walks are to be at the same time you prepare the rest of the garden. Then, after you have finished planting the borders and beds, recultivate the paths as necessary and plant the ground cover, working backwards toward the entrance of the garden as you would when waxing a floor. (Plant the paths last so that you will have a place to walk while you plant the beds.)

You may want to enclose the herb garden with a wall or hedge. Fragrant hedges such as lavender, rosemary, or germander (see pages 27-29) can be planted around the perimeter of the garden to give it a feeling of intimacy, or you can use lower growing hedges such as boxwood and dwarf sage to border the paths. Be sure you allow enough space for the hedge plants to grow without encroaching on other herbs that are next to them.

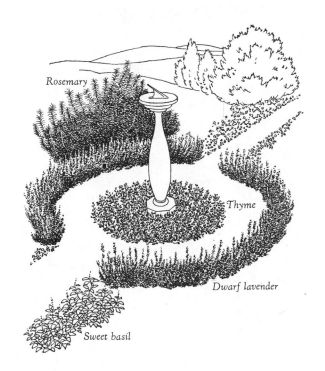

SUNDIAL AND HERBS are not restricted to formal land-scapes. Here they are an interlude in a casual garden path.

SEMI-FORMAL PLANTING of herbs is illustrated by this spoke garden. The semi-circle is divided into sections by bricks buried in the ground. Chamomile forms the hub and the hedge is germander.

HERBS IN THE LANDSCAPE

There is no rule saying that herbs must be grown only in formal gardens, or that they must be set off from the rest of the landscape. Tradition seems to have disassociated herbs from other ornamental garden plants and modern landscape designs, but most herbs are really free-wheeling plants that can be used in many ways in the landscape.

Some herbs, such as the santolinas, grow dense and compact, just right for tucking into corners or filling open spaces between other plants. Low creeping herbs such as the ground cover thymes, mints, and sweet woodruff can be used to cover small areas, and to grow over hard structural lines or pavement edges. Or, they can be used alone or with other plants as a ground cover over large areas.

Interplanted with other perennials in a border, herbs can create interesting patterns and textures. Shrubby herbs such as tansy and borage can be interplanted with woody ornamentals and perennials. Lemon verbena, the taller varieties of rosemary, bush germander, and other tall herbs are good background plants in flower borders, and can be planted against fences to give some texture to their flat surfaces. Many of the culinary herbs such as parsley, dwarf sage, winter savory, and chives can be low edgings and foreground plantings in front of taller perennials.

Herbs can also provide bright spots of color in the landscape. Yarrows, tansy, purple basil, and lavender make colorful plantings, and there is a wide variety of gray foliaged herbs such as artemisias and santolina which can be used as landscape highlights, foils for colorful flowers, or to moderate the greens of other plants.

Herbs can grow between paving stones of a patio, or in hard to fill spaces between a wall and walk. One of the advantages of planting herbs in areas such as these is that they are tough and usually require only a little care.

Aggressive, rambling herbs such as catnip, some of the mints, and lemon balm are usually too wild and spreading for a formal or tidy garden, but are perfect in more informal gardens where they can wander freely among other plants, softening transitions and filling in empty spaces.

Other herbs are compact and have a distinguished, neat appearance. Many of the santolinas and the germanders can be clipped and shaped. Other herbs such as trailing rosemary will soften the lines of a garden when trained to spill over walls or flow gracefully between other plants.

Several herbs are at home in woodsy landscapes. Chervil and sweet cicely like shade or sun-filtered shade, and their fernlike foliage goes well as a background for other ferny woodland plants. Sweet woodruff and the mints spread along the ground and make good fillers in shady gardens.

SHADED by tall tree, parsley, sweet woodruff, and mint do well. In the background grow dill and angelica.

HILLSIDE LANDSCAPE contains many culinary and ornamental herbs, plus rock garden plants and stones.

GRAY-LEAFED santolina has a thick, clumpish growth form that adapts beautifully to the contours of this rock. The flower heads are golden yellow.

YARROW and white alyssum fill this colorful border. Yarrow colors range from red to yellow and white.

WOOLLY THYME provides a shag carpet ground cover for blue scillas in a corner of this garden.

WOOLLY THYME *grows in a low spreading mat of fuzzy leaves that make it a good filler or ground cover. Here it has crept over the edges of a raised bed and grows in the cracks between the stones of a wall.*

CREEPING THYME *is a tough herb that can withstand moderate foot traffic. Here it is rooted between paving stones of a terrace where it offers its fragrance when stepped on.*

CHINESE CHIVES *have white flowers and thick clumps of leaves that make a good seasonal border for tall annuals.*

SPILLING *over a wall, trailing rosemary softens flat surfaces and provides cascades of blue color.*

HARD-TO-GARDEN *space between this rock retaining wall and walk is neatly filled with thyme. Other herbs could be planted between the rocks in earth-filled crevices.*

BORDER *of scented geraniums and lavender cotton (in center) is not only attractive but also inviting for passersby to pinch and sniff their various fragrances.*

GREEK YARROW (Achillea ageratifolia) *with its silvery green, paddle-shaped leaves grows in a low mat that adapts well as a ground cover or filler in woodland gardens. Here it spills over a bulkhead log.*

SANTOLINA'S GRAY FOLIAGE provides a good filler beneath these nandinas and contrasts strikingly with their green and reddish leaves.

YEAR-ROUND GREENERY in warm winter climates is one of the features that make rosemary a highly usable landscape plant. Here creeping rosemary fills the spaces between carolina cherry trees in this desert landscape.

LOW MAINTENANCE ground cover for sunny, dry locations, creeping thyme produces a blanket of white flowers during the blooming season.

Herbs for Ground Covers

Several herbs can become attractive ground or bank covers. Drought resistant herbs such as rosemary and thyme perform well in dry, sunny areas that would not support more sensitive plants. Sweet woodruff and most of the mints do well in moisture and shade and make attractive ground covers in woodland landscapes. Some others—notably chamomile—can be mowed and walked on as a lawn substitute.

Rosemary. Rosemary makes a 2-6 foot ground cover depending on the variety and how it is trimmed. *R. officinalis* 'Collingwood Ingram' grows to about 2-2½ feet tall, and the gracefully curving branches spread 4 feet or more along the ground. Rich, bright blue-violet flowers cover most of the foliage in the summer, making it a colorful, tall, bank cover. *R. o.* 'Lockwood de Forest' resembles the prostrate variety but has lighter foliage and bluer flowers. *R. o.* 'prostratus' or dwarf rosemary hugs the ground closely, usually growing only 1-2 feet tall and spreading to 4-8 feet. The stems of this variety will spill nicely over ledges and walls.

All of these rosemaries can endure hot sun and poor soil, but good drainage is a must. Once established they need little or no watering except in the desert. Feeding and excess watering result in rank growth and woodiness,

and eventual death. Control their growth by frequent tip pinching when the plants are small. Older plants will need occasional light pruning to keep them looking neat; make all cuts to the side branches. For a ground cover, set small rosemary plants about 2 feet apart. For quick growth, feed lightly and head back new growth periodically to encourage bushiness.

Thyme. Like rosemary, thyme grows in warm, light, well drained soil and full sun. It can withstand a fair amount of neglect. As ground covers, the thymes grow lower than the rosemaries and have more matted foliage. Woolly thyme (*T. lanuginosus*) forms a flat to undulating mat— 2-3 inches high—of dense, small woolly leaves. This species is best for covering small areas (including difficult ones) but is not for large areas because the plants tend to become rangy in winter. Caraway scented thyme (*T. herba-barona*) forms a thick, flat mat of dark green, ¼ inch long leaves that have a caraway odor. *T. serpyllum* or creeping thyme forms a thick mat 2-6 inches high and will withstand occasional foot traffic.

As a ground cover, plant the thymes 6-12 inches apart in the fall or spring and restrain them as needed by trimming back the growing tips.

Germander. Prostrate germander (*Teucrium chamaedrys* 'prostratum') is a tough herb that likes sun and heat and will endure poor, rocky soils. It grows 6-12 inches high and spreads to about 2 feet.

DROUGHT-RESISTANT *creeping rosemary is a natural ground cover for this sunny, dry bank. Once established, plants need only minimal watering even in hot summer climates.*

FRAGRANT PATHWAY of silver thyme flows from patio down a slope to meadow and lawn, is tough and durable.

DITTANY OF CRETE is distinctive ground cover for sunny locations. Foliage forms a deep mat of woolly leaves.

SWEET WOODRUFF makes a lush ground cover in shady, moist locations. Profuse summer blooms are white.

TINY PURPLE BLOSSOMS turn this ground cover of creeping thyme into a sheet of color in spring and summer.

CONTAINED in an open square in this patio, spearmint holds its own against a husky passion vine.

Shady areas that receive little sun are sometimes difficult to cover. Sweet woodruff (*Asperula odorata*) is a low-growing herb with spreading stems 6-12 inches high. The whorls of rich green leaves are attractive in woodland settings. It loves shade and moisture and grows best in a rich soil.

Corsican mint (*Mentha requienii*) is another woodsy ground cover with interesting foliage. It grows only ½ inch high, and the tiny round bright green leaves have a mossy effect. It spreads at a moderate to rapid rate if given shade and plenty of water.

There are several herbs that can be grown as lawn substitutes. Chamomile (*Anthemis nobilis*) is a traditional ground cover for paths and walkways in herb gardens. It forms a soft-textured, spreading, 3-12 inch mat of light green, finely cut leaves. If mowed occasionally, it can be kept short enough to serve as an aromatic lawn. Plant divisions 12 inches apart in full sun or very light shade and water moderately.

Cotula (*Cotula squalida*), though not an herb, often is substituted for chamomile in most Western States. Its growth habit is similar to chamomile and the leaves are soft, hairy, and fernlike with a bronzy green color. It is sometimes called brass buttons because of the yellow, buttonlike flowers that can be kept mowed down for a flat surface.

Herb Hedge Plantings

Some of the fragrant herbs can grow as borders, edgings, and low hedges. Others that aren't fragrant also make good low hedges because they have interesting foliage or ornamental gray leaves. Boxwood, though not an herb, is the traditional edging in knot and formal herb gardens.

Lavender. Probably the most ideal fragrant hedge is English or true lavender (*Lavandula spica*) or spike lavender (*L. latifolia*). Bushy, with narrow gray-green foliage, it grows 3-4 feet high. Wonderfully fragrant flowers, lavender in color, grow in spikes at the ends of straight stems one foot or more in length. You can use the flowers in sachets, potpourris, and arrangements.

Even though you may not want to gather the flowers for their fragrance, cut the stems after blooming to keep the plants tight and bushy. Keep the sides trimmed for a formal appearance. About every 3 or 4 years, take cuttings, root them, and replace old, woody plants with the new rooted cuttings.

Dwarf lavenders, some of which grow to about one foot high, make tidy little hedges or edgings. *L. stoechas,* sometimes called Spanish lavender, grows about 1½-3 feet high and has deep purple flowers in dense spikes. *L. spica* 'Munstead' is a miniature English lavender, about 18 inches tall and earlier blooming than the species.

Lavender hedges are beautiful in themselves, wonderfully effective along brick, stone, or gravel paths, and are compatible with many flowers, especially iris, roses, carnations, garden pinks, gypsophila, nepeta, and regal lilies. The spiky blossoms of lavender add a sharp accent to perennial borders.

Rosemary. Upright species of rosemary (*Rosmarinus officinalis*) are rangy and grow to about 2-6 feet high. Rosemary makes a higher, broader hedge than lavender. The gray-green foliage and stems carry a strong, resinous, piney scent. In mild winter sections along the Pacific coast, the soft lavender-blue flowers bloom through the winter and into early summer. In the Northwest, rosemary usually doesn't bloom until April. A little more touchy than lavender, rosemary cannot be counted on to come through extremely severe winters. Prune it after blooming to encourage new growth. Upright varieties such as 'Tuscan Blue' should be planted 15 inches apart for a hedge.

Santolina. One of the most useful low hedges, santolina or woolly cotton (*Santolina chamaecyparissus*) is more pungent than fragrant. Ordinarily it grows as a spreading plant 18 inches to 2 feet high, but it looks attractive when clipped to make a tight little hedge or edging about 10-15 inches tall. Although santolina's short, toothed leaves are

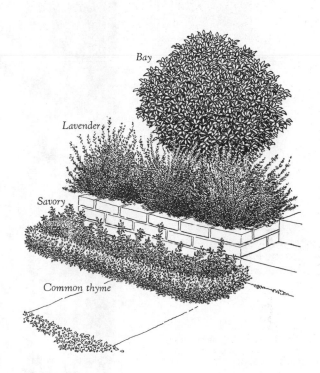

BORDER *of savory and thyme is backed by a lavender hedge which screens a bay tree-shaded patio.*

FRAGRANT HEDGE *of lavender is good choice for bordering a garden walk. This border is of English lavender.*

HEDGE *of common rosemary screens entryway of house from the street. Plants were set 15 inches apart and are trimmed occasionally to keep growth neat.*

SANTOLINA BLOSSOMS *are bright yellow and button-like, appear only on hedges that are not closely trimmed.*

best described as gray-green, the plant takes on an almost white appearance when full grown and is a good night time plant for corners of paths and near garden steps. Some gardeners do not consider attractive the bright yellow, button-like flowers and prefer to cut them off before they bloom.

Another species, *S. virens*, is similar except for its deep green leaves.

Use santolina in the same way you would lavender. In size it is the equivalent of boxwood for edging formal beds in old-fashioned knot and herb gardens. Beds planted tightly with bright colored flowers look neat behind clipped santolina.

Germander. Though it is not fragrant, bush germander (*Teucrium fruticans*) is suitable for growing as a medium to tall hedge. It is 4-8 feet tall and each plant can grow up to 6 feet wide. It makes a gray-green, silvery hedge and can be clipped into various shapes for formal appearance or allowed to grow more coarsely for casual gardens.

Another species, *T. chamaedrys*, is lower, 1-2 feet tall and spreading to about 2 feet with dark green leaves and many branching stems. For a neat appearance, shear plants back once or twice a year to force side branching.

SILVERY WHITE FOLIAGE
*of this bush germander hedge acts
as a white "curb" along the gravel
path at night. When trimmed as
this one is, germander can be
kept at about 2 feet.*

*INFORMAL SCREEN of bush germander separates this courtyard from the rest of the garden. Allowed to grow
naturally with only minimal pruning, germander will reach 4 or 5 feet. Set plants 3 or 4 feet apart.*

FIVE HERBS—*parsley, rosemary, chives, mint, and tarragon—grow well in this planter. In mild winter climates, the box can be moved to a protected corner.*

❧ HERBS IN CONTAINERS

There are many attractive ways to grow herbs in containers, and there are many advantages to this kind of growing. A few small plants often can be more interesting in containers where they can show off than in the garden which might tend to engulf them. If your garden is small or if the herbs will not readily fit into your landscape, planting them in containers is an easy solution. Containers also can be brought indoors or moved about the garden as the sun changes position or as frosts threaten. Almost every herb can be grown in a container if it is planted in proper soil and given the proper sun and water; herbs with tap roots are the only possible exceptions. If you do pot them, be sure that the container is deep enough for the full grown root.

There are many kinds of suitable containers, ranging from ordinary clay pots and wooden planters to unusual and distinctive jars and bowls. Choose one that will fill the needs of the herbs and enhance their beauty.

The container must meet only a few basic requirements, the first and most important of which is drainage. There should be holes or slits in the bottom of the container to let water flow out so that the soil and roots won't become

DWARF ROSEMARY *grows well in containers. This basket-shaped pot is just one of many kinds available.*

waterlogged. A good container should also be able to withstand constant moistening and drying out.

Most plant containers sold will meet these standards, but do remember them when devising your own containers or choosing one that is not specifically designed for plants.

Any container you use must be clean. Scrub off old potting soil, moss, and stains with hot water and a stiff brush. Rinse or wash new containers in hot water before planting in them.

Unglazed clay flower pots are the most versatile and widely used garden containers. They are available almost everywhere and relatively inexpensive. The earthy, old-world look of unglazed pots goes well with any of the herbs. They come in brick red, yellowish tan, off white, chocolate brown, and in a variety of sizes and shapes.

You can plant one or more herbs in a single pot or grow several in a large one. Or, arrange the containers together—a convenient way to grow several herbs near one another that have different culture and water requirements.

Terra cotta strawberry jars are distinctive and well suited for a variety of herbs. They come in sizes ranging from 12-18 inches high with six to eight planting pockets at various levels along the sides. Herbs with a tendency to trail are attractive in the pockets while upright herbs or a few showy, large-leafed types such as geranium or mint can crown the top. There also are flatter versions with pockets on only one level.

Clay pots also come in many glazes and colors. If you choose one of these, however, be sure that the color or glaze doesn't clash with the herb's foliage or the surroundings in which it will be placed.

Wooden containers have a mellow appeal, and the color and texture of wood blends well with almost all garden features. These containers can be used as window boxes, on patios, or as part of the landscape. You can buy many types of planters and tubs, or you can easily design and make your own. As an example, a 32-inch long planter box that is ten inches deep and ten inches wide will hold about half a dozen herbs such as rosemary, sweet marjoram, oregano, thyme, parsley, and chives.

Large wooden boxes and tubs that remain in one place for long periods of time without being moved should have cleats or runners underneath them, permitting free water drainage and air circulation to prevent decay.

Hanging containers can display herbs dramatically. A group of culinary herbs hanging outside a sunny kitchen window or door is very convenient when you want a sprig or two while cooking.

Trailing herbs such as rosemary, thyme and dittany are naturals for hanging containers. Others such as basil, marjoram, and sage will also begin to spill over the sides as their stems grow long.

CONVENIENT and attractive, hanging pot holds basil, marjoram, and thyme in pockets, chives and parsley on top.

STRAWBERRY JAR OVERFLOWS with scented geraniums and rosemary; culinary herbs are in the side pockets.

SHALLOW POTTERY BOWL is filled with silver thyme, tri-color sage, orange mint, and apple mint. Bowls such as this one come in many sizes with flat or rounded sides; be sure you choose one with holes for drainage.

OREGANO BONSAI makes a unique container plant. Plant had grown in the garden 10-15 years prior to training.

Many clay containers are designed with hooks or other provisions for hanging them. If not, they can be suspended in a net, macrame piece, or by leather thongs.

Though most herbs are sun lovers, benefiting from about eight hours of sun each day, in the garden their roots are insulated from overheating because the plants' leaves shade the soil area in which the roots grow. Containers do not always provide this insulation from heat because the sides are exposed to warm sunlight and drying air. Both of these can quickly dry out the soil, roots, and the plants. A simple way to minimize this danger is to locate your container-planted herbs where they will receive shade during the hottest part of the day. Herbs such as mint, parsley, and sweet woodruff prefer less sun than the others and should be given shade for most of the day with perhaps an hour or two of exposure to the sun in the morning or late afternoon.

When you plant several herbs in one container it is best to plant together only those that require similar amounts of water, sun, and soil conditions. Check the herbal on pages 56-79 for the needs of the herbs you want to grow. The more vigorous herbs such as mint and lemon verbena should be planted separately or kept well controlled as they tend to overcrowd most others.

ROSEMARY *variety 'Angustifolia' was trained as a standard by removing side shoots along a single stem.*

TERRA COTTA FISH *holds a healthy plant of marjoram. Pot can be moved easily around the patio for best sun.*

COLORFUL NASTURTIUMS *have been placed on a low brick wall where foliage can spill over sides of container.*

HANGING OUTSIDE *the kitchen door, rosemary, lemon thyme, and chives are right at hand for a cook to pick.*

Watering

There are no special techniques for watering herbs in containers. If you water from the top, use a garden hose and low pressure or a watering can that has a sprinkler head. Apply water to the container until it begins to run out of the drainage hole in the bottom. Never use a strong spray from a hose. It would wash out soil and expose roots or damage stems. Place the container in a dish or saucer if excess water would harm the floor. During cooler weather, be sure to empty the dish after each watering so that roots and soil won't become soaked.

Another way to water is to set the container in a dish or saucer of water for an hour or so and allow the soil to absorb moisture. When the soil's surface appears damp, the plant has enough water.

Check container plants about every other day—every day in hot weather especially if the container is small or porous. If the soil just beneath the surface is dry, water the herbs. Never allow soil in a container to dry out completely. If it does the root ball will shrink, and when you water it will just run over the surface of the soil, down the inside and out the drainage holes without being absorbed. If the soil gets in this condition, loosen the dry soil ball with a stick or screw driver, then soak the soil thoroughly for several hours.

A simple method for determining when a clay pot needs watering is to gently tap the side of the pot with a stick of wood: a dull thud indicates moist soil, no more water is necessary; a clear tone like that of an empty pot indicates a dry soil mass that has contracted and allowed an air space between the soil and the pot itself.

Potting and Transplanting

To get new plants from nursery containers into their permanent containers or to transplant them from one container to a larger one, place one hand on top of the container that the plant is in with its stem between your index and second fingers. Then, grasp the bottom with the other hand, invert the pot, and tap the rim sharply against the edge of a bench or table to loosen the root ball. Lift the pot away from the plant, steadying the roots with the hand the plant is in. (If the soil isn't moist enough, it will fall to pieces.)

A well-drained porous potting soil mixed with a little bonemeal is the best potting medium for herbs. If you mix your own, use equal parts of topsoil, sand, and ground bark, leaf mold, or peat moss and 1 teaspoon of bonemeal per 6-inch pot. Fill the container so that when you place the plant inside, the surface of its root ball will

NEW PLANTS *from the nursery (shown above) can be transplanted into new containers illustrated at right.*

come to within about an inch of the pot's rim. Firm the soil in well around the root ball and water thoroughly so that both the new soil and the root ball are evenly moist. It is a good idea to set newly potted plants in the shade for a few days until they become adjusted to their new environment.

If, after four to six months, you notice that a plant is no longer growing vigorously and seems to wilt quickly, despite what should be adequate watering, or if the roots begin to twine out of the drainage hole, remove the plant from its container and see if the roots have formed a tight network around the outside of the soil ball. If so, gently loosen the root system, remove old soil that is loose, and repot the plant into a larger container as described above.

Many herbs such as chives and mint grow larger by sending up new sprouts or runners. This new growth can be separated from the main root system as described on page 45 to give you small new plants for other containers or the garden. Dittany and sage tend to layer themselves and each rooted stem can be cut apart from the main plant to produce several plants and reduce the size of the original.

Seedlings from the garden can be dug up and potted as soon as they have formed four true leaves. Leave some of the garden soil around the roots to form a root ball; place the plant into a container; then fill in around the roots with potting soil according to the directions given above.

TAP the bottom of the pot gently against a bench or table to loosen the root ball from the container.

SUPPORT the plant and roots with one hand, invert pot, and slowly pull it away from the root ball.

POT BOUND established plants must have their roots loosened before replanting in a larger container.

POSITION plant so that top of root ball comes within an inch of new container's rim, then fill around it with soil.

🌿 GROWING HERBS INDOORS

Growing herbs is not limited to the garden. Most herbs that you can grow outdoors in containers also can grow indoors. If you live in an apartment and have no outdoor gardening space or if you want the flavor and fragrance of fresh herbs during the winter months, simply plant your favorites in containers and bring them inside. A pot of culinary herbs sitting on the kitchen windowsill will always be at hand when you are cooking. Pots of scented geraniums or mints growing in the living room will be a refreshing reminder of outdoor gardens and summertime.

Many perennial herbs such as the scented pelargoniums, lavender, and rosemary are tender where winters are severe and should be dug up from the garden, put into pots, and wintered indoors if the plants are not too large. It is even easier to grow these perennials outdoors in containers, then move them inside when winter approaches. Annual herbs can be started from seeds in containers indoors in the late fall or winter as described on pages 40-42 to provide fresh seasoning for winter cooking. Herbs that grow easily indoors are noted in the herbal beginning on page 56.

How Much Light?

Most of the culinary and ornamental herbs should get at least 5 hours of sun each day. A few, however, (such as chervil, lovage, lemon balm, the mints, sweet cicely, and sweet woodruff) will grow well without direct sunlight as long as they receive good light.

A sunny window is a good location as long as the reflected heat is not too intense. If you don't have an available window that is exposed to direct sunlight, choose a spot that will provide the herbs with good light, and move the plants into the sun for a few hours whenever possible.

Fluorescent Lamps. An alternative to growing herbs in natural light is to raise them under fluorescent lights. Several manufacturers of fluorescent tubes produce types specifically designed for illuminating plants; these emit light in wave lengths favorable for plant growth. These special tubes are available in the usual fluorescent lamp sizes from 24 to 96 inches long and will fit into ordinary fluorescent fixtures. A standard fluorescent light arrangement consists of two of these tubes of whatever length you desire plus a reflector which is a canopy that throws

CLAY PIG with curly parsley growing on his back is a decorative ornament for any kitchen shelf, besides being handy for garnishing food. Parsley is easily grown from seeds sown directly in the container.

STOVESIDE BOX neatly holds six potted culinary herbs; chives, oregano, garden sage, pineapple sage, parsley, and coriander. Gravel in the bottom of the box absorbs drainage of excess water.

light back onto the plants. You may have to do a bit of experimenting to determine the best intensity and length of exposure for your indoor herbs, but as a starting point give them 14-16 hours of light each day with the lights anywhere from 12 to 18 inches above the top of the pots.

Temperature and Humidity

Herbs will be happy in the same indoor atmosphere that you prefer to live in yourself. Difficulties that arise with herbs indoors are often due to air that is too hot and dry, as is the case in many kitchens. Normal room temperature is best (around 70°). The herbs will survive nighttime drops in temperature as long as they do not reach freezing levels, but any prolonged periods of dry heat will be detrimental. Humidity should be between 30 and 50 percent. If it is less in your indoor growing area place a bowl or dish of water near the herbs: as it evaporates the water will moisten the air directly around the plants. You can check humidity with a small hygrometer often available in hardware, craft, or sporting goods stores.

Fresh, moving air is essential for indoor herbs. If the plants are next to a window, leave it open a crack for an hour or so each day, but be careful not to put them in a direct draft—especially during the winter. Generally, any room that is not stuffy with stale air will be satisfactory.

Watering Guidelines

Check indoor herbs daily for soil moisture. If the soil just beneath the surface is dry, water the plants with room temperature tap water as described on page 34. The herbs will also appreciate having their foliage sprinkled with water to freshen them.

Be sure to rotate the containers frequently, regularly, and always in the same direction so that all sides of the plants get approximately equal exposure to light and air. Without this turning, the herbs will grow more exuberantly on the side exposed to the strongest light, while the shadow side will grow more slowly or the foliage there may wither and drop.

Pest and Disease Tips

Though it is usually supposed that the oil in their leaves makes herbs resistant to diseases and repels most insect pests, you would be wise to take a few precautions to assure their health. Herbs transplanted from the garden and brought indoors should be checked for aphids and red spider mites. If you find either on your plants, use a weak solution of yellow naphtha soap and water to control both pests on those herbs that you will use in cooking. Malathion is good for controlling aphids on non-culinary herbs.

GROWING, HARVESTING, AND CURING are steps prior to using herbs. Here are sage, chives, and marjoram with stems of dried rosemary, parsley in a jar for storage, and ground sage in a mortar and pestle.

General Techniques for Propagating, Using

THERE ARE several ways of getting herbs into the garden; the choice depends mostly upon your needs. The easiest methods are either to buy them as small plants from the nursery or to raise them from seeds. Planting seeds will provide you with enough herb plants not only for use in cooking, but also for fragrant arrangements and ornament. If you need only one or two plants for occasional kitchen use, to fill a spot in the garden, or to decorate a container, it will probably be more convenient to buy the small herbs that most nurseries stock during spring and summer.

Many perennial herbs can be propagated from stem or root division so that once these herbs are in your garden it is easy to increase your supply.

GROWING HERBS FROM SEEDS

For the most common culinary and ornamental herbs, seeds are available at nurseries. Mail order seed houses and herb growing friends are good sources for less common varieties and specialty herbs. Avoid buying herb seed packets that contain mixed seeds. The seedlings will be difficult to tell apart from one another when they come up, and the more aggressive kinds will tend to crowd the weaker or slower-to-germinate ones.

You can plant seeds directly in the garden or in containers. If you sow seeds in prepared garden soil, plants will sprout up, right where you want them, and you can thin them in place without need for further transplanting. With container sowing, you can get a jump on the growing season by starting seeds indoors while it is still too cold for outside planting; and you can start slow-to-germinate perennial seeds without tying up valuable garden space.

Planting Seeds in the Garden

You can sow any herb seeds in the garden as soon as the danger of frost has passed and the soil has begun to warm up. The best time is when the soil is crumbly and not too wet.

Seeds that have a long germination period (such as rosemary and lavender) also can be sown in the fall and will come up nicely the following spring; this avoids a long wait for seedlings to appear during the growing season. Plant these slower seeds before autumn frosts begin but late enough in the season that they will not come up before winter, only to be killed when cold weather does settle in. Be sure to check the seed packets for any specific planting directions for your region.

Preparing the Soil. First choose a place in your garden where the herbs will thrive. Most herbs like a sunny location, although a few such as the mints and chamomile prefer some shade, especially during the hottest part of the day. The individual herb descriptions (pages 56-79) will give you cultural information for the herbs you want to grow.

Almost all herbs—even the mints—like well drained soil and will not grow well if their roots are constantly moist. To provide this, turn the soil to a depth of about one foot (roughly a spade's depth) and break up the clods. If the soil drains poorly, add organic matter—such as peat moss, leaf mold, wood by-products, or compost—to lighten it. At this point it is also a good idea to check the soil's pH with your county agriculture agent. He will be able to tell you if the soil in your area is likely to be alkaline, neutral, or acid and can suggest measures to raise or lower the pH according to your needs. Herbs such as thyme, lavender, rosemary, and burnet prefer neutral to slightly alkaline soil; others, like angelica, prefer a soil that is slightly acid. Check the specific needs of the herbs you are planning to grow in the descriptions on pages 56-79.

Sowing the Seeds. After preparing the bed as described above, make shallow scratch lines with a rake as a guide for sowing. Place the seeds into the furrows and cover lightly and evenly with soil. The smaller seeds can be mixed with sand to assist even distribution. The instructions on the backs of the seed packets should tell you how thickly to sow them and how deeply they should be covered; twice the diameter of the seeds is a general guide for covering. Mark and label the rows so that you will know later what seeds are planted and where they are.

After covering the seeds with soil, firm the bed down with a board or your hand to assure good contact between seeds and soil. Moisten the bed with a fine spray of water, but be very careful not to dislodge the seeds. The soil should be kept moist but never soggy.

If hungry, seed-eating birds frequent your garden, you would be wise to cover seeded areas with mesh screening until seeds germinate.

The germination period for the seeds is usually stated on the back of each seed packet. An average time for annuals is 12 to 14 days; perennials usually take a little longer, perhaps 3 weeks to a month.

After two pairs of true leaves develop, thin the crowded areas by pulling out the small, weaker seedlings, or by transplanting the healthier ones. In hot areas leave plants close enough together that the foliage will always shade the soil. Remember that many culinary herbs have flavor almost as soon as they sprout, so you can use those seedlings you have thinned from the rows in seasoning foods.

Broadcasting is a good planting method if you want clumps or large plots of a single herb rather than rows of it. Prepare the soil as you would for row planting, but instead of placing the seeds in rows scatter them evenly over the area by hand or with a seeder. Then cover and water as described for planting in rows.

Planting Seeds in Containers

There are a number of advantages to starting seeds indoors in flats or other containers. Annual and perennial herbs that take a long time to germinate can be started indoors late in the winter and will be small plants ready for transplanting into the garden by spring. Indoors you also have more control over atmosphere and soil conditions which is an advantage if the growing season is short or if the climate in your area is temperamental.

Anise, chervil, coriander, dill, and fennel do not always transplant successfully because they form long tap roots. For the greatest success with these herbs, transplant them while plants are small enough that you can dig the entire root system without breaking the tap root.

Containers and Growing Mixtures. You can start seeds in just about any sort of container. Cut-down milk cartons, pots, and flats are all good as long as they are clean and provide adequate drainage. Commercially made flats and pots usually have drainage holes or slits built into them. Punch drainage holes into the bottoms of homemade containers.

Use a propagating mix that is loose, drains well (won't cake like clay), yet holds moisture. Equal parts coarse sand, peat moss or fine ground bark, and garden loam make a good basic mix. Sift the components through a ¼-inch mesh screen to remove rocks and soil clods, or pick them out by hand. If you do not mix your own soil, use a good commercial seeding mixture. Some gardeners prefer to start seeds in a sterile medium such as vermiculite.

Sowing. Fill the flat or container with your soil mixture to within about ½ to ¾ inch of the top and firm it down with a block of wood or the palm of your hand. Mark off rows about 2 inches apart with a piece of lath or a pencil, pressing ⅛ to ¼ inch into the surface.

Place the seeds into these furrows and cover with soil to whatever depth the packet says or approximately twice their diameter. Most fine seeds should not be buried but pressed into the soil surface instead. Firm the soil down so that the seeds come into good contact with it.

Water the container carefully with a fine spray, being careful not to wash the seeds out of place. A small syringe or a fine mist from a misting nozzle is best for top watering. Another good method—especially if you have planted seeds in small containers—is to soak the bottom of the container in a dish or sink filled with water so that moisture will be drawn up into the soil by capillary action. With either watering method—top or bottom—keep the soil moist but not soaking wet.

Label the containers or rows and put a piece of wet burlap or newspaper over the soil surface to retain mois-

SCREEN COVER *over this plot of newly planted seeds protects them from seed eating birds that may visit the garden.*

PREPARE FLATS FOR SEEDS *by filling them with soil and firming it down well. Next, mark shallow rows for the seeds with a piece of lath or ruler. At top of photo is box for sifting soil and a board for firming it down.*

ture. Place the containers in a fairly warm location—65°-75°—until germination begins.

The seeds will not need light until they have sprouted but they will need fresh air to prevent mold and fungus from forming. Lift the cover for an hour or two every day or so to let fresh air reach the soil surface.

After Germination. When seedlings begin to germinate, remove the covering and move containers to a cooler location (60°-70°) where they will receive good light but not direct sunlight which can burn them. Turn the container every day or so (and always in the same direction) to give the seedlings equal exposure to light on all sides.

Damping off is the only problem you may encounter at this stage. It is a decaying of the stems at soil level caused by a fungus that thrives when there is too much water in the soil and the plants are not given enough fresh air or the temperature is too warm. To combat damping off, use a commercial fungicide; those that contain captan or dexon give the best results.

When seedlings have two sets of true leaves they are ready to be thinned. If you planted in flats or other temporary containers this is also the time to transplant into larger or permanent ones which will give the herbs room to develop.

The new containers should be filled with a slightly richer soil mixture than the one in which the seeds were started. A good mixture is two parts garden loam, one part coarse sand, and one part sifted peat moss or finely ground bark. Space seedlings in the new container about 1½ inches apart and water them carefully from the top or the bottom as described above.

Several weeks later, when the plants have put on enough growth so that their leaves touch those of their neighbors, they are ready to be planted into their permanent locations. (See page 34 for transplanting instructions.) If you intend to transplant the herbs into the garden, place the flat outdoors in the shade for a few hours each day during the week before scheduled transplanting; this will minimize the shock of transition from indoors to outside.

A fairly recent innovation in seed growing is packages containing seeds which are already planted in small cup-size containers of growing medium. The cups are made of a humusy material and are simply planted in the ground when the seedlings grow large enough to be set out. When planted in soil the container will decompose, providing food for the roots and room for them to expand. Be careful, however, not to let the cups dry out at any time: If they do, they can inhibit root spread or act as a wick and steal moisture from the soil they contain.

HERB GROWING KITS are inexpensive and include seeds planted in small humus containers, a plastic greenhouse, and instructions. All you do is water and plant into the ground or pots when the herbs have sprouted.

CUTTINGS or "slips" can be taken from tip growth by bending stem sharply against your fingernail as shown above.

LENGTH OF CUTTINGS should be 3-6 inches. Remove foliage from lower half of stem before planting.

Fertilizing Guideline

Contrary to some popular beliefs, herbs will appreciate well balanced fertilizer in moderation; soil that is too poor will produce foliage that is sparse and has poor flavor. When fertilizing, however, remember that a too rich soil will generate lush growth with only small concentrations of oil in the leaves.

PROPAGATING THE PERENNIALS

There are several ways to increase perennial herbs once they are established in the garden or in containers. You should find that all methods are easy to do and give a high percentage of success.

Stem Cuttings

Rooting stem cuttings or "slips" is perhaps the simplest method for propagating perennial herbs and often is faster than growing the same herbs from seeds. Herbs such as feverfew, lavender, lemon balm, rosemary, pineapple sage, winter savory, and southernwood grow well from stem cuttings. Mints are particularly responsive, rooting in only a few weeks, so if the practice is unfamiliar to you try a favorite variety of this herb first.

The cuttings can be taken any time in the spring or summer during the active growing season; take them from healthy, well-established plants. Strong, new tip growth makes the best cuttings. Do not take the soft or forced growth that results from too little light, weak shoots from the center of the plant, or exceptionally vigorous growth with thick stems. Stems that snap when bent sharply— rather than those that bend without breaking—give the best results.

Make the cutting just below a leaf bud or node, using a sharp knife, razor blade, or shears to make the cut. The cuttings should be between 3 and 6 inches long and have good foliage on the upper end.

Between the time you cut the stems and plant them, keep the cuttings out of the sun between two layers of damp cloth or paper towels to prevent them from drying and wilting.

A good propagation soil mixture is two parts sand and one part vermiculite. If you are rooting a large number of cuttings, a nursery flat makes a good propagating bed. For just a few, you can use a clay pot or an empty coffee can. Be sure that whatever container you use has provisions for drainage.

Thoroughly moisten and drain the mix, then fill the container to within about ½ inch of the top, firm well, and level the surface. Before inserting the cuttings, strip the leaves from the lower ½ or ⅓ of each stem, and dip the cut end in a hormone powder to stimulate root growth. Place the defoliated ends into the soil about ½ or ⅓ the length of the stems and water gently to settle the soil. Cover the cuttings with a plastic bag or an inverted glass jar to keep the soil moist and the humidity high. Occasionally raise the jar or remove the cover to admit fresh air and to prevent molds and fungus from forming. Set the cuttings where they will receive good light but not direct sunlight, and turn the containers to give the cuttings equal light on all sides.

The quicker rooting herbs such as lemon balm, thyme, and basil usually take from 4 to 6 weeks to form roots. Herbs with especially woody stems such as rosemary, myrtle, artemisia, santolina, and germander may take several months.

When roots have formed, the foliage will gain a bright green color and, although there probably will not be any new leaves, the cuttings will then be ready for transplanting into individual pots that are about 3-4 inches in diameter. Be gentle when you lift newly rooted plants and, if you can, leave some of the original propagating mix around the roots (or put a little bit in the planting hole in the new container). Until new growth starts, keep the herbs out of the sun and the soil moist.

As soon as roots begin to poke through the drainage hole in the individual pots the plants are ready to be transplanted into larger containers or into the garden. Follow the transplanting procedures described on page 34.

Layering

Layering is perhaps the simplest method of increasing many of your perennial herbs such as mints, sage, thyme, winter savory, marjoram, lemon balm, santolina, and rosemary. It is a simple method in which branches are brought into contact with the soil, causing them to take root while still attached to the parent plant. Many herbs, in fact, layer themselves naturally from branches that creep along the ground.

Select a vigorous branch growing close to the ground or one that is flexible enough to bend down to the soil. Bend it down and select a section about 12 inches from the stem tip and just below a leaf node. Directly below this part, dig a shallow hole, and mix the soil with equal parts peat moss or ground bark and sand: It is here that you will bury the stem so that it will form roots.

LAYERED ROSEMARY branch can be separated from main plant and transplanted into new location or container.

ROOTED ROSEMARY cutting is ready for transplanting even though no appreciable new growth has formed.

On the underside of the branch at the part that will be buried, make a slanting cut half way through (on slender stems simply scrape away the outer layer of the surface) and put some hormone powder on the cut or scrape to stimulate root growth. Next, bend the branch down into the hole and anchor it in place with a heavy wire loop or staple. Bring the end of the branch to a vertical position and stake it upright. Finally, fill in the hole, firm down the soil, and water thoroughly. To keep the soil firm and help maintain moisture, place a brick or stone on the surface directly above the layered stem section.

When layering in the fall in cold winter areas, spread a mulch over the layering to protect it, leaving only the tip and several leaves exposed.

Roots may form in as little as 6 weeks for many herbs. Check for root growth by carefully removing the soil from around the stem. When roots are well established, sever the stem from the parent plant and move your new plant to its garden location or container.

Root Cuttings

You also can take root cuttings from any plant that sends up new stems from its roots. This includes catnip, horehound, rosemary, savory, myrtles, sage, lemon verbena, germanders, thymes, lemon balm, artemisia, and tarragon.

Select roots 3/16 to 3/8 inch in diameter from vigorous plants and cut them into pieces 1-3 inches long. Fill a box or flat to within about 1 inch of the top with light garden loam and place the cuttings 2 inches apart in a horizontal position on top of the soil. Cover with about ½ inch of additional soil, and water thoroughly. Cover with glass or newspaper and place in the shade. When new growth and leaf buds appear, remove the covering and transplant each cutting into individual small pots, or transplant them into a deeper flat about 6-8 inches apart.

Root Division

Each year the roots of many perennials grow and spread, sending up new growth that increases the size of the plant. These new roots are capable of becoming independent plants when pulled or cut apart from the parent. Chives and tarragon are examples.

The best time to divide is in the autumn or early spring, when plants are not forming new growth. Dig the herb up from the ground and simply pull or cut the root clump into sections. After dividing, replant the sections into the garden or containers as soon as possible, and keep the soil moist until the plants have adjusted.

POT BOUND CLUMP of chives has mass of tangled roots that can be separated into several separate plants.

DIVIDE CLUMP of chives into smaller groups of plants (shown here) or into individual plants, then repot in new soil.

LEAVES of most culinary herbs can simply be picked or cut as soon as the plant is large enough not to miss them. Cutting the tips will encourage bushy growth and side branching.

 ## HARVESTING HINTS

Once the herbs are growing happily in your garden or containers they will provide a source for culinary adventure, flavorful teas, and fragrant combinations. It is in these uses that they distinguish themselves from other plants and truly show their qualities as herbs. First, however, the leaves and seeds must be harvested.

Using Fresh Herbs

The leaves of most culinary herbs such as basil, chives, marjoram, mints, parsley, rosemary, sage, and thyme have enough flavor throughout the growing season that you can harvest them to use while fresh at any time. Pick only healthy green leaves — not yellowed or dead ones. Be very careful, however, that you don't injure the plant's growth by pulling off too many leaves from one stem or plant—particularly with young ones.

When the herbs are large and full enough, you can cut sprigs from the ends of stems. This is called pinching. It also stimulates new growth, causing the plant to become fuller and bushier than it would if allowed to grow unchecked. If you want flowers for bouquets or seeds for

planting the following spring, let a few stems grow and mature into blossoms.

Though you will enjoy using the herbs fresh, you will probably also want to dry some for winter cooking and for making fragrant preparations such as potpourris and sachets. Keep this in mind while picking in the summer so that you will leave enough foliage for a large fall harvest.

How to Pick for Drying

Although herbs may be cut and used fresh at almost any time, the main harvest of leaves and seeds for preserving comes during the blooming period. Herbs tend to lose some of their flavor during the drying process. The best time to harvest them for drying is when the flowers first open. It is then that the oils which give each herb its distinctive flavor and aroma (held in tiny glands in the leaves) become most concentrated. The only exceptions are: hyssop, lavender, rosemary, and thyme—cut them when the blooms are fullest; and sage—harvest it when the buds first appear.

Choose a sunny, dry morning just after the dew has dried from the leaves but before the sun is hot. Some annuals bloom early in the summer, and if you do not cut

SEEDS ARE HARVESTED by cutting off the entire seed head at the stem. Harvest when they ripen and turn brown, but before they drop to the ground and are lost.

them back too much this first time they will regrow enough by fall for a second harvest. If you are harvesting annuals in the fall you can simply cut them to the ground.

Shrubby perennial herbs (such as lavender, marjoram, and rosemary) should be cut back annually after blooming to encourage compact growth; this is also an easy way to harvest leaves and flowers for drying. Cut back about half the length of the current year's growth.

Harvesting Seeds and Flowers

Some of the herbs such as anise, caraway, coriander, and dill produce seeds that are tasty on pastries and other dishes. As soon as the seed heads or capsules turn brown—but before they fully ripen and scatter the seeds—cut the entire seed head or stem into a paper bag. Do this on a warm, dry day.

Seeds to be used for future planting should be harvested when the seed capsules begin to yellow and are about ready to drop off.

Flowers for drying, fresh arrangements, and potpourris can be cut with a knife or pruning shears. Choose newly opened ones that are bright and fresh.

 ## CURING THE HERBS

There are several ways of preserving herbs. Drying is the best known method and works well with just about all herb leaves, flowers, and seeds. A few herbs—such as basil, fennel, dill, chives, and burnet—do not dry well, and their flavor lasts better if the leaves are frozen or packed in salt.

Perennials such as mints, rosemary, and thyme can provide you with fresh leaves throughout the year in areas where winters are mild. In cold winter areas, bring plants indoors for a continual supply of fresh leaves. With these perennial herbs you only need to preserve the leaves for recipes specifically requiring them dried.

Methods for Drying

All methods of drying herbs are simple and just involve various ways of exposing the leaves, flowers, or seeds to warm, dry air. The most important thing is that air be able to freely circulate around the drying herbs to absorb their moisture in such a way that the oils are not destroyed. Sunlight will damage the leaves and their flavor so do not expose them directly to the sun. A warm, even temperature is best. If you dry herbs outside, remember to bring them inside at night so dew won't dampen them.

The most picturesque drying method is to tie the ends of the stems together into a bunch and hang them upside down. This works best with herbs that have long stems, such as marjoram, sage, savory, the mints, and rosemary. To harvest herbs for bunch drying, cut the branches fairly long and do not remove the leaves. Rinse in cool water and discard any leaves that are dead or have lost their color. Then, tie the ends of the stems together into small bunches and hang them upside down in a warm dry room where they will not be exposed to direct sunlight. Air must circulate around all sides of the leaves, so do not hang the bunches against a wall.

If there is a chance that dust will collect on the herbs while they are drying, place them inside paper bags and gather the top of the bag around the tied end of the stems so the leaves hang freely inside the sack. Cut out the bottom of the bag and punch air holes in the sides for ventilation.

After a week or two the herbs should be crackly dry, and you can take them down. Carefully remove the leaves, without breaking them, from the stems. Some leaves such as rosemary become hard and sharp, so you might want to wear gloves when you strip them from the stems.

Seeds, large-leafed herbs like basil, or short tips of stems may be difficult to tie together for drying, but you can dry them easily on a screen or tray.

The three drying boxes in the photograph are designed to be stacked one on top of the other. They are easily constructed from pieces of 1 by 2-inch lumber with window screen for the bottom. The boxes are about 8 inches long by 7 inches wide — large enough to hold a sizable quantity of herbs. The bottom box sits on two small strips of wood so that air can pass freely through all the boxes. Similar drying screens or trays can be made to any convenient size, and cheesecloth can be used instead of window screen.

In preparing to dry leaves on trays, you can either strip them from their stems or leave them attached, but spread only one layer of leaves on each tray. If you try to dry too many at one time, air will not be able to reach all of them evenly, and they will take longer to cure.

Every few days, stir or turn the leaves gently to assure even and thorough drying. It should take a week or so for them to dry completely, depending on the temperature and humidity. When the leaves are crisp and thoroughly dry, remove them from the racks.

Seed heads can be spread in a thin layer on the trays or screens and dried in the same fashion (and under the same conditions) as leaves. When the seeds are ready to shake loose from the dried seed capsules, carefully rub the capsules through your hands. A gentle breeze or the air from

TO DRY LONG-STEMMED HERBS, such as rosemary, tie together with string into bunches and hang upside down.

DRYING BOXES are ideal for curing small quantities of herbs. Screens allow for air circulation.

a fan will help waft away the chaff, leaving the seeds.

Flowers can be dried by hanging or spreading them on racks or trays as described above. Again, the sun is harmful and will bleach their color and destroy their fragrance. The best method for drying whole flowers is to cover them with borax or fine sand as described on page 54.

Curing With Salt

You can cure some herbs in salt as is frequently done with basil. Rinse the leaves in water and let the water dry, or blot the leaves between two pieces of cloth or absorbent paper; then pick the leaves from their stems. Into a jar, first pour a layer of non-iodized table salt, add a layer of the leaves, and then another layer of salt. Fill the jar in this manner, alternating layers of salt and leaves, until the jar is full. Press the leaves and salt down firmly, cover tightly, and store the jar in a dark place.

Use the salted leaves as you would fresh herbs, but be sure to rinse them well first in clear water or else allow for the extra salt when using the leaves in a recipe.

Freezing Fresh Herbs

Some of the more tender herbs such as fennel, burnet, dill, tarragon, chives, parsley, and basil can be frozen. This is also a good way to save herbs that you have picked to use while fresh but do not need at the moment. Harvest and wash the herbs as you would for drying, but leave the foliage on the stems. Tie a string or length of thread around the stems and blanch them in unsalted boiling water for about 50 seconds, holding onto the string so you can remove them quickly. Next, cool the herbs by dipping them in ice water or cold tap water for a few minutes; then remove the leaves from their stems and place leaves in freezer bags or foil. Label the bags and put them in the freezer.

If you chop the leaves before packaging, they will be ready to use as soon as you take them out of the freezer. The blanching is not really necessary for all of the herbs. Dill, chives, and basil can simply be washed and frozen as they are freshly picked.

Freezing is a very handy method if you put only small quantities in each wrapping, about as much as you would use in a recipe.

To use frozen herbs, simply take them out of the freezer and add them still frozen to the food you are cooking. They must be defrosted first when used in salads and other cold foods.

Storing the Dried Herbs

Store the thoroughly dried herbs in airtight containers that are labeled for easy identification. Leaves that were left on the stems during the drying process can be removed before storing. Do this gently, being careful not to break them.

Leaves will retain their flavor longer if you leave them whole and break them up only as you use them. If the container is made of glass or any other transparent material, it should be kept out of the light in a cool, dark cupboard.

During the first week after packaging the herbs, occasionally look to see if any moisture or condensation has formed on the inside of the containers. If moisture does appear, the herbs are not quite fully dry and should be taken out and dried for another day or two to prevent them from decaying in storage.

Seeds also should be stored in airtight containers. Both heat and light will destroy the viability of seeds you intend to plant and the flavor of culinary seeds. Put them in a dark, cool place where the temperature is even, such as in the refrigerator.

FOR STORING HERBS, jars and bottles often can be decorative, but they must have airtight stoppers.

🌿 HERB TEAS

Among the most popular herbal preparations are the herb teas. They are simple to make and can be brewed and enjoyed whenever the mood strikes you for exotic flavored refreshment. If you put the herbs for teas into simple jars or bottles they can make attractive gift items.

In years past, herbal teas seem to have had a much greater role in everyday living. They were not only popular for their flavor, but were taken quite often medicinally to cure coughs, sore throats, fevers, and headaches.

Preparing an herbal tea is easy, but you'll have to experiment a bit to get the right strength for your taste. Begin by trying about a teaspoon of the dried herb—a little more if you are brewing from fresh herbs—for every serving (about 6 ounces) of tea. (The herbs can be crushed first to help release their flavor.) You can put the herb directly into the teapot or into a tea ball; then, boil the necessary amount of water and pour it into the pot in which the herbs have been placed. The pot should be preheated with boiling water.

Generally, teas should steep not less than 10 minutes; if they are steeped too long, however, they may become bitter. If you want a stronger flavor after trying the amount of herbs recommended above, use more herbs rather than steeping them longer.

The teas are usually best if milk or cream is not added.

A few can be sweetened with a little sugar or honey and lemon, but before adding a sweetener, taste the brew first to see if you like it just the way it is.

The taste of various herb teas is one thing that few people will agree upon: Many teas are flavorful; some are strong and medicinal; and all are nearly impossible to describe in a few words. A few of the more popular ones are brewed from chamomile, lemon verbena, mint, rose hips, rosemary, and thyme, but when it comes right down to it, you can brew a tea from almost any of the culinary herbs you choose. Health and specialty food stores often have a wide selection of herbal teas, so if you aren't growing an herb that you'd like to make a tea from you often can buy it already prepared for brewing.

🌿 HERBED BUTTER

Herbs blended with butter make a tasty seasoning for any food that you usually would accompany with butter. Spread herbed butters on vegetables, over French bread, or melt the butters on plain broiled steaks, fish fillets, hamburger patties, or poached eggs. Rosemary butter is good on lamb chops, steak, and fish. Oregano butter is a perfect partner for roast corn or broiled tomatoes. Use your imagination when trying other herbs such as tarra-

HERBAL TEAS shown here are (clockwise from left): sassafras (bark); rose hips (fruit); chamomile (flower); sassafras; and bay (leaves). In attractive containers herb teas make interesting gifts.

FLAVORED BUTTERS are good with many different foods and can be made with nearly any culinary herb. Simply whip the herb with butter in a blender, or grind the herb and beat by hand into butter until fluffy.

gon, marjoram, thyme, chervil, or a blend of several herbs.

To make herbed butter simply combine butter or margarine with the herbs you have selected in a blender and whirl until smooth. Or, crush the herbs first in a mortar and pestle, then beat together with the butter until smooth. Cover the butter and refrigerate. A good starting ratio to use is 2 tablespoons of dried herbs (½ cup fresh herbs) per ½ cup butter.

Flavored butters are not intended for long-time storage. For best flavor, plan to use them within a week or two.

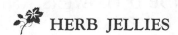 HERB JELLIES

Rather interesting flavor harmonies can be made by blending your herbs with various fruit juices into jellies. The process is simple and the result is a deliciously different spread for breakfast toast and hot breads, or a companion for entrees and desserts.

Follow these directions for each jelly: In a large kettle combine fruit juice (or water) and the herb; heat to scalding. Remove from the heat and let stand for 15 minutes. Strain the liquid through a fine cloth or several thicknesses of cheesecloth. Return the liquid to the kettle, add lemon juice, food coloring (a few drops at a time until the desired shade), and pectin. Place over high heat and stir until the mixture comes to a full boil. Stir in the sugar and return to a rolling boil; boil for 1 minute if you use 1¾-ounce package of pectin (or 2 minutes for 2 ounces), stirring constantly. Remove from heat, skim off the foam, immediately pour into sterilized jelly glasses, filling one at a time, sealing as filled with scalding lids and ring. Invert the jar to coat top surface with hot jelly, then place right side up to cool. This will make 6 glasses (6 oz. size).

Here are a few possibilities:

Thyme-grape jelly

3	cups grape juice
1	teaspoon dried thyme
2½	teaspoons lemon juice
1	package (1¾ or 2 oz.) powdered pectin
3½	cups sugar

Sage-cider jelly

3	cups apple cider
1½	tablespoons dried sage
1	package (1¾ or 2 oz.) powdered pectin
4	cups sugar

Rose-geranium jelly

3	cups water
1	cup washed and stemmed rose geranium leaves
1	package (1¾ or 2 oz.) powdered pectin
4	cups sugar
	red food coloring

Marjoram-grapefruit jelly

¼	cup fresh marjoram or 1 tablespoon dried
3	cups unsweetened, canned grapefruit juice
1¼	tablespoons lemon juice
1	package (1¾ or 2 oz.) powdered pectin
4	cups sugar

Mint-cider jelly

1	cup spearmint leaves
3	cups apple cider
	few drops of green food coloring
1	package (1¾ or 2 oz.) powdered pectin
4	cups sugar

HERBED VINEGARS

By adding herbs to vinegar you can give extra flavor to any stew, vegetable dish, sauce, or soup that normally calls for vinegar in the recipe. Basil vinegar gives a morning glass of tomato juice a little zest, tarragon vinegar can be added to a pot of beans, and mint vinegar is a compatible seasoning for lamb chops and ham—to cite just a few of the many possibilities. Try a combination of seasoned vinegars such as garlic and tarragon, onion and basil, or garlic and marjoram in French dressing.

Herbed vinegars are easy to make, and you can use either fresh or dried herbs in their preparation. Put ½ cup

CRYSTALLIZED VIOLETS are both decorative and flavorful, add a touch of the unusual to cakes and ice cream.

of slightly crushed fresh leaves of the herb you choose (or 1 tablespoon if the herb is dried) into a jar with 2 cups of white, cider, or wine vinegar. (This will give you about 2 cups of herbed vinegar.) Let it stand for about 4 days; then strain the liquid, discarding the herbs, and bring the vinegar to a boil. Remove the vinegar from heat and pour it into hot, sterilized jars. Cap them tightly and store in a cool, dark shelf or cupboard. The vinegars are best used within six weeks.

If you plan to use the vinegars as gifts and want them to look attractive, you might want to place a whole sprig of the herb into the bottle before you cap it.

CANDIED FLOWERS AND LEAVES

The leaves and flowers of many herbs can be candied or crystallized into delicate, sweet, sugar-crisp decorations just like the French confections sold in specialty stores. Candied violet blossoms, for example, can be pretty toppings for fancy desserts and ice cream; crystallized sweetheart roses can be used to decorate special occasion cakes or frosted petits fours—or they can float in champagne and other sparkling beverages. Other herb flowers and leaves such as mint and the blue, star-shaped borage

ROSE BLOSSOMS *are here being rolled in colored sugar after having been dipped in sugar syrup.*

HERBED VINEGARS *in clear glass bottles contain sprigs of the flavoring herb for easy identification.*

blossoms can be used as similar decorations.

Always pick fresh leaves and new buds as soon as they open. The only special ingredient you'll need is gum arabic powder, available at most drug stores. (Ask the pharmacist—he usually can order it for you if he doesn't have it in stock.)

How to Crystallize Flowers and Leaves

In the top part of a double boiler, combine 2 ounces (5½ tablespoons) of gum arabic powder with 1 cup of water. Place the mixture over boiling water, and stir until the gum arabic is dissolved. Let this cool to room temperature.

Wash the blossoms or leaves (start with about 2 dozen) with a gentle spray of water. Trim the stems near the base of the buds and leaves and stick a toothpick into the bud as a replacement. Allow the blossoms or leaves to drain thoroughly.

Dip one blossom or leaf at a time into the cooled gum arabic solution to coat all surfaces. Stick the end of the toothpick into a base of styrofoam or clay to hold the blossom upright, then let each one dry thoroughly for about 1½ hours. The finished blossoms will be tissue-like and brittle, so handle them carefully.

Prepare colored sugar by adding about 8 drops of food coloring (to make the sugar the color of the blossoms or leaves you are using) to one cup of sugar. Stir until the color is distributed throughout the sugar. Pour onto waxed paper and let stand 1 hour.

Combine 2 cups of sugar, one cup of water, and 2 tablespoons white corn syrup in a pan and bring to a boil. Cook until the mixture reaches the soft ball stage (234 degrees on a candy thermometer). Stir in a few drops of food coloring to make the syrup the same color as the colored sugar. Cool the syrup until you can hold your hand on the bottom of the pan comfortably. (If the syrup is too hot, the petals and leaves will turn brown after dipping.)

Dip the blossoms or leaves into the cooled syrup one at a time, making sure that each petal is coated. Allow excess syrup to drain from blossoms, then roll them in colored sugar. Again, stick the toothpicks that hold the flowers into a styrofoam or clay base to allow the coating to dry partially—about 15 minutes. When all blossoms have been dipped and sugar-coated, sprinkle the remaining colored sugar into a shallow pan that has been lined with waxed paper. Carefully remove blossoms from their toothpicks and place them on the sugar; allow them to dry there thoroughly for 8 hours or longer. Finally, inspect each blossom to be sure it is completely dry, then store them in airtight containers until you are ready to use them.

Collecting the Ingredients

Preserved in jars or bowls, potpourris are delightful, old-fashioned combinations of fragrant flower petals, herbs, and spices mixed together. When the lid is removed, the sweet garden scents are released for your enjoyment. The aroma of a potpourri depends only upon your imaginative blending of various flower petals, leaves, and oils. Many can be kept for years without losing their fragrance.

The main ingredient of many potpourris is dried flower petals and fragrant leaves. The flowers of roses, lavender, lemon verbena, and rose geranium hold their fragrances best. Old-fashioned roses such as cabbage and damask, kazanlik, rose de Provins, and moss roses are traditional favorites, but one of the fragrant modern types such as Etoile de Hollande, Crimson Glory, Texas Centennial, Chrysler Imperial, The Doctor, Radiance, Lowell Thomas, Tawny Gold, Tiffany, and Sutter's Gold may also be used.

Although jasmine, mignonette, violet, and hyacinth have marvelous fragrances while the flowers are fresh, they lose their scent rapidly when dried.

The dried leaves of lemon verbena, the mints, and other herbs such as rosemary, thyme, basil, and marjoram furnish other fragrances that you can use.

Bits of citrus peel with the white membrane removed, cloves, allspice, ginger, nutmeg, and the crushed seeds of anise, caraway, cardamom, and coriander, and oils extracted from rosemary, bitter almond, citrus, and other fragrant plants can also be added. Spices, herbs, and oils that you don't have can be obtained from the seasoning shelves at grocery stores, herb shops, and drug stores. (Do not use the extracts on the spice shelves in grocery stores.) Never add too many different kinds of fragrances, especially oils, as they tend to counteract one another.

Fixatives. To preserve and blend the aroma of the leaves and flowers, a fixative is added to the potpourri to absorb the vital oils and retard their evaporation. There are many different fixatives, some of which will contribute to the final fragrance. Orris root powder (from the root of the Florentine iris) and gum benzoin are usually the most readily available at health food stores, pharmacies, and herb shops. If none of these places have them, ask a pharmacist to order them for you.

Fixatives generally come in a powdered or ground form; either will do but the powdered form tends to coat the inside of clear glass containers and mar their transparency.

Other fixatives include calamus powder, a derivative from the root of sweet flag; storax, a balsam from the bark of *Liquidambar orientalis* or *Styrax officinalis;* and animal derivatives such as musk, ambergris, and civet. One ounce of fixative for every 2 quarts of petals is the proportion generally used in most mixes.

You can start gathering the flowers for the potpourri as soon as they open, and continue adding to the collection through the blooming season. Gather the fragrant and colorful flowers for drying on a warm, sunny day as soon as the dew has dried. Select blooms that have freshly opened, not old ones ready to drop their petals.

To dry the fragrant blossoms, remove petals from the flowers and spread them out thinly on newspaper, tissue paper, or—best of all—on a wire or cheesecloth screen as described on page 48 for drying herb leaves. Place the petals in a warm, dry, shady spot where they will dry quickly and without appreciable loss of their fragrance.

Since many fragrant flower petals lose their color during the drying and curing processes, other whole dried flowers often are added. Bee balm, cardinal flower, calendula, elecampane, nasturtium, yellow primrose, delphinium, larkspur, violets, pansy, jasmine, and bachelor buttons all retain their colors well when they are dried.

Dry whole flowers (which are attractive in glass containers) by spreading about ½ inch of borax or fine sand in the bottom of a box. Place the whole flowers face down, then carefully sift more sand or borax over them until they are covered. Keep the box in a warm, dry place until the flowers are completely dry— usually

POTPOURRIS COMBINE fragrances of herbs, flowers, and other essential oils into long lasting aromatic blends.

in about 2 weeks. Then gently remove flowers from sand and store them in a dark place so they will retain their colors until you want to use them.

Assembling the Potpourri

There are two ways of making potpourri: the dry method and a more complicated wet process.

Dry potpourri. After the petals, herbs, and leaves are crisp and dry, mix them up thoroughly in a large bowl and blend in the other spices and oils, adding them a little at a time until the desired fragrance is obtained. Then add the fixative.

After you have blended all ingredients together, store the potpourri in glass jars or other interesting containers and cover tightly. Choose glass bottles and bowls that will show off the colors.

Here is a typical dry potpourri recipe.

3	quarts rose petals (from pink and yellow roses)
1	pint lemon verbena
1	pint rose geranium
½	pint pennyroyal
½	cup lavender flowers
1	cup bergamot
1	cup rosemary
6	tablespoons orris root (coarse)
5	tablespoons gum benzoin (crushed)
½	cup orange peel (shredded and dried in a slow oven)
1	tablespoon crushed cloves
1	tablespoon coriander seeds (optional)
2	tablespoons Tonka beans (cut)

Mix the first 9 ingredients together. Be sure that the petals and leaves are "chip" dry. Toss lightly as you add the remaining ones—a little at a time until the desired fragrance is attained. Let the mixture stand in sealed containers for 5 to 6 weeks, shaking them occasionally to blend the fragrances.

Wet potpourri. When the flower petals are partially dry and feel leathery, pour them into a large, straight-sided crockery jar in ½-inch layers alternated with sprinklings of coarse salt. Pack the salt and petals firmly and when the jar is ¾ full, place a weight on the top to press them down. Do not place metal directly on the petals; instead, use a ceramic weight or place a plate on top of the mixture and set a metal weight on the plate. As soon as moisture drawn out by the salt rises to the top, stir up the petals

and let them cure for ten days. During this period they should not be disturbed. The petals will form a moist cake; when you are ready to do the final blending, break it into small pieces.

Since the salt removes the color from flower petals, this potpourri is best put into opaque jars. The fragrance of wet potpourri is very heavy, so these mixes usually are kept in tightly covered containers and opened when their fragrance is desired.

The following recipe is representative of wet potpourri preparations.

2	quarts leathery-dry rose petals, lavender flowers, and herbs (basil, marjoram, pineapple mint, rosemary)
	Coarse, uniodized salt
½	vanilla bean, crushed or chopped
1	tablespoon crushed nigella seeds
½	tangerine skin, chopped and with the white membrane removed
2	heaping tablespoons mixed spices (cinnamon, mace, nutmeg, ginger)
12	whole cloves, crushed
1	ounce fixative (orris root, powdered gum benzoin, or ½ ounce each)
5	drops of essential oil (rose geranium, patchoule, or orange blossom but never more than one)

Mix the rose petals, lavender flowers, and herbs together and pack them in salt to make a moist cake as described above. When the mixture is cured, break up the cake very finely and blend it with the vanilla bean, nigella seeds, tangerine skin, and spices. Add the fixative and oil and pack the potpourri in opaque containers.

Sweet herb potpourri. Here is a dry potpourri variation using only herbs to help you get started on a creation of your own.

1	pint pineapple mint leaves
1	pint apple mint leaves
¼	cup each spearmint, Salvia clevelandii, sweet basil, Oswego tea, sweet marjoram, sweet woodruff, lemon balm, lemon verbena, pineapple sage, clary sage, and rosemary
3	tablespoons lavender blossoms
2	cardamon seeds and pods, crushed
10	coriander seeds, crushed
1	teaspoon sweet basil
1	ounce powdered orris root for a fixative

Combine the ingredients and let them blend for a couple of weeks in a large sealed container before packaging in glass jars.

Favorite Herbs and How to Grow Them

In the three previous chapters we dealt with the history, culture, propagation, and uses of herbs. In this final section, 49 of the more popular and useful herbs are individually illustrated and described in detail. Many of them are culinary herbs that you can grow either in the garden or indoors and whose leaves or seeds can be used to season foods. Others possess fragrances which will give sweet aromas to potpourris and dried arrangements. A few of these herbs find their only contemporary use as highly ornamental landscape plants.

For each herb covered in the following pages you will find a description of its principal species and varieties, their foliage and flowers, growth habits, cultural requirements, means of propagation, harvesting information, and suggestions for uses in the garden, in cooking, or in fragrant preparations. In addition, each description contains a paragraph which explains the plant's history, folklore, and early uses.

These herbs are arranged according to their common names, the botanical name of each following in parentheses. For convenience, a quick reference list of vital information is provided at the top of each description.

ANISE (*Pimpinella anisum*)

Plant: annual

Height: 2 feet

Soil: light, fairly rich

Exposure: full sun

Propagation: seeds

Uses: culinary

You will find two types of leaves on the anise plant. Those which grow thickly at the base of the stem are bright green, oval, and have toothed edges. On the stems, rising above the basal leaves, appear smaller, elongated leaves—each divided into three segments. The tiny flowers are white and grow at the top of the 2-foot stems in thick, umbrellalike clusters.

Anise is one of the oldest known herbs, having been mentioned in ancient Egyptian records. Originally from Greece and Egypt, it traveled north with the Romans to Europe and England and is one of the first European herbs to have been planted in America. Anise was used by the Romans to make a rich cake, eaten at feasts, which is thought to be the prototype of our wedding cake.

Best growth is in light, fertile, well drained soil. Start plants from seeds as soon as the ground warms up in spring. Because plants have a tap root they do not transplant well after established, so start them where they are to grow, or transplant while seedlings are still small.

Anise is most famous for the licorice flavor of its leaves and seeds. Use the leaves fresh in salads, and the seeds for flavoring cookies, pastries, and confections. Anise is also used to flavor many liqueurs.

ANGELICA (*Angelica archangelica*)

Plant: biennial

Height: 4-6 feet

Soil: moist, slightly acid

Exposure: semi-shade

Propagation: seeds

Uses: culinary

Although angelica is a biennial herb—growing the first

year and flowering the second—it will continue to live for several more years if you clip off the flower stems before they bloom. The yellowish green, tropical looking leaves are large, becoming about 2-3 feet long, and are divided into 3 leaflets with toothed edges. Greenish white flowers bloom in umbrellalike clusters at the ends of the bloom stalks which are 4-6 feet tall, hollow, and stiff.

As the name implies, angelica has religious associations. It is said that an angel presented the plant to man as a cure for the plague, and 15th and 16th century herbalists recommended eating or chewing the roots as a cure for a number of diseases. It was also believed that angelica would protect against witchcraft and evil spells. In Lapland and parts of Germany, angelica is often carried in processions while a verse is sung whose origins are pre-Christian and so old that the participants do not know its entire meaning.

Angelica likes moist, rich soil that is slightly acid, growing best in semi-shade. It can be grown from seeds, but they must be sown within a few weeks after ripening or they lose their ability to germinate. If you allow seeds to ripen on the stems, they will self sow readily. You also can propagate angelica from root cuttings.

The roots, leaves, and stalks of angelica have a number of uses. The stems can be candied and used to decorate cakes and pastries, and can also be jellied. You can even eat the boiled roots and stems like celery. The seeds and an oil made from the stems and roots are used as a flavoring in many liqueurs such as vermouth, chartreuse, and Benedictine, and the seeds also can be brewed into a tea.

Harvest the stalks in the second season and the seeds as soon as they are ripe.

BASIL (*Ocimum basilicum*)

Plant: annual

Height: 1-2 feet

Soil: moderately rich, moist

Exposure: sun

Propagation: seeds

Uses: culinary

The basils are attractive annual herbs with a sharp, spicy flavor and long history of use. There are several species, but the plants most commonly grown for culinary and ornamental values are *O. basilicum* and its varieties.

Sweet basil (*O. basilicum*) grows to about 2 feet high

and has shiny green leaves that are 1-2 inches long. Small white flowers grow in spikes at the ends of the stems. If the stem tips are pinched out frequently, sweet basil will grow bushy and full, making it an attractive border plant. This species is the most popular one for cooking. The variety 'Dark Opal' won an All-America bronze medal for its decorative, purple-bronze foliage and spikes of small lavender-pink flowers.

Bush basil (*O. b. minimum*) has more branches and a more compact growth than sweet basil. The leaves are much smaller, and the edges curl inward toward the center vein. It grows to about 1½ feet tall.

Basil has a rich history, but the stories about it often are contradictory. In Italy, basil is associated with sympathy and compassion which is supposed to arise between those who wear sprigs of it. In other countries, basil is a sign of love and devotion between young couples. A few 16th and 17th century herbalists have a different idea of its nature and associate it with scorpions and poison: One recommended placing basil leaves on the bites and stings of poisonous snakes and insects, saying that "Every like draws its like"—certainly the opposite of its ability to attract two lovers.

All basils can be grown in full sun or semi-shade and a warm, moderately rich soil. They should not be fertilized as flavor is likely to be sacrificed for lush growth. Water regularly to keep growth succulent and the leaves fresh. Indoors, basil requires sun and should be pinched occasionally to keep growth bushy. Basil grows readily from seeds sown in the spring as soon as the ground is warm.

The leaves have a spicy, clove-like flavor that is an excellent complement to such foods as eggs, cheese, fish, poultry, stuffings, salads, meats, and spaghetti. It is especially good in tomato dishes. Use either the fresh or cured leaves. Preserve them by freezing or packing in salt. (You might try chopping the fresh leaves and adding a little olive oil before freezing them.)

BEE BALM (*Monarda didyma*)

Plant: perennial, hardy to —20°

Height: 3 feet

Soil: moist, fairly rich

Exposure: sun, partial shade

Propagation: cuttings, division

Uses: fragrance, culinary

Bee balm, also called Oswego tea and bergamot, is a native American plant but is named after Monardes, a 16th century Spanish botanist. A leafy, bushy perennial, its branching stems grow to about 3 feet high; clusters of scarlet flowers which are attractive to hummingbirds rise from colored bracts at the ends of the stems during summer and early fall. There are several named garden varieties: 'Cambridge Scarlet,' a fiery red; 'Croftway Pink,' a lavender-pink; and 'Granite Pink,' a lovely clear pink. The flowers and foliage have a strong minty aroma.

Plants grow well in sun or shade, but the mats of shallow roots are very invasive, so use it where you can contain its growth easily. Cut plants back periodically to keep them compact, and divide them every 3 or 4 years.

Use bee balm leaves for potpourris and tea, and to flavor jellies and fruit salads. The flowers are attractive in fresh arrangements.

BORAGE (*Borago officinalis*)

Plant: annual

Height: 1-3 feet

Soil: dry, somewhat poor

Exposure: sun or shade

Propagation: seeds

Uses: culinary

This distinctive annual has branching stems that grow from a single tap root to about 1-3 feet tall. The gray-green leaves are 4-6 inches long and, like the stems, are covered with bristly hairs. Borage produces beautiful star shaped, peacock blue flowers that nod downward in leafy clusters at the tips of stems. Plants are best used where they can be seen close up: in border plantings and in containers, for example. They take up a lot of room in the garden and don't transplant well, so space plants a generous distance apart.

Medieval literature states that borage is supposed to give strength of heart, courage, and joyfulness to anyone who eats the leaves or drinks wine in which the flowers or leaves are floating: appropriately, astrologers placed it under the rulership of Jupiter—the largest planet, named after the king of the Roman gods—and the zodiac sign of Leo, which is symbolized by the lion.

In the past, borage has been used to help cure fevers; but the descriptions of its virtues by early writers are contradictory, some saying that it is cooling and others that it is spicy hot. You'll have to try it yourself to find which is correct.

Borage likes sun or filtered shade, slightly poor soil, and only moderate amounts of water. It grows readily from seeds sown in the spring and will reseed itself so easily that it can become a weed in mild climates.

The leaves have a cucumber-like flavor and can be used in salads and pickling or can be cooked as a green and eaten like spinach. Cut the flowers just after they open for use in arrangements or for color in potpourris: They also can be floated in iced drinks or candied (described on page 52) and used to decorate cakes and ice cream.

BURNET (*Sanguisorba minor*)

Plant: perennial, hardy to —30°

Height: 1-2 feet

Soil: average, well drained

Exposure: sun

Propagation: seeds, division

Uses: culinary

Small burnet or salad burnet is a perennial, most of whose leaves grow alternately along the stems and close to the ground in rosettes about 8-12 inches high and 1½-2 feet across. The leaves consist of rounded toothed leaflets that are in opposite pairs along the leaf stalks. The flower stems grow upright from the middle of the rosettes to about 2 feet and bear clusters of unusual thimble-shaped rose colored flowers. Burnet makes an attractive ground cover (if the flower stems are kept cut back) and a good container ornamental.

Burnet was valued most for its herbal healing qualities. It was supposed to slow the flow of blood in small veins, and there is a story that King Chaba of Hungary used it to heal the wounds of 15,000 soldiers after a great battle. A tea made from the leaves is supposed to have been taken by American Revolutionary soldiers the night before entering battle so that, if wounded, they would not bleed to death.

Grow burnet in any well drained soil and in full sun. It does, however, require routine watering. It grows easily from seeds, and if the flowers are allowed to mature they will self sow almost too freely. You also can divide the clumps if you want more plants.

Salad burnet has a fresh, pleasant, cucumber-like flavor. The leaves can be added to salads, iced drinks, vinegar, butters, and cream cheese. Use only the fresh, new leaves.

CARAWAY (*Carum carvi*)

Plant, biennial, hardy to —30°

Height: 2 feet

Soil: neutral, well drained

Exposure: sun

Propagation: seeds

Uses: culinary

During its first year, caraway grows about 8-15 inches high and then reaches about 2 feet in the second. In the second year, flat, umbrellalike clusters of greenish white flowers appear on the stems above the foliage and in mid-summer ripen into seeds—after which the plant dies. Foliage is delicate and lacy, like that of carrots.

A native of southeastern Europe and western Asia, caraway has been in use for thousands of years. Seeds which are believed to be caraway have been found in ancient lake villages in Switzerland. Ancient Greeks prescribed caraway seeds for bringing color back into the faces of girls with pale complexions. The seeds were eaten by the Romans to relieve indigestion, and its roots were cooked and eaten like carrots or turnips. Now, caraway is used as a flavoring in Kummel and foods such as rye bread.

Start caraway from seeds sown in the fall or spring where they are to grow. This herb thrives in well drained, neutral garden soil and full sun. In cold climates, protect yearling plants with a mulch during the winter.

Harvest the seeds when they have ripened but before they fall to the ground. They can be used to flavor pickles, cabbage, Brussels sprouts, cauliflower, and rye bread; or serve them in the traditional old English manner—in a small dish along with baked apples.

CATNIP (*Nepeta cataria*)

Plant: perennial, hardy to —30°

Height: 2-3 feet

Soil: moist, rich

Exposure: sun, partial shade

Propagation: seeds, cuttings

Uses: fragrance (for cats), tea

Catnip is a perennial herb native to Europe but now found wild in many parts of the United States and often considered a weed here. Plants are 2-3 feet tall with branching, upright stems similar to the mints. The leaves are heart-shaped with pointed tips and toothed edges, green on the upper sides and a grayish color underneath. Colorful spikes of lavender or white flowers bloom in June at the tips of the stems. With age, plants can become scraggly and should be cut back each year after flowering to keep looking neat and to prevent them from spreading. Another species of nepeta is *N. mussinii* or cat mint. It grows in soft undulating mounds 1-2 feet high and has ½-inch lavender-blue flowers in loose spikes at the ends of the stems. For a ground cover, set plants 12 to 18 inches apart.

Give catnip a light, rich soil in sun or partial shade, and moderate moisture. Sow seeds in early spring or late fall. You also can propagate by root division in the fall or spring, by layering, or from stem cuttings.

In the past, catnip has been used for treating hysteria, nervousness, and headaches. The aroma of the leaves has a well known effect on almost all cats, making them kittenish and playful. Because cats are tempted to play in plants of catnip growing in the garden, you may want to protect young seedlings until they are large enough so they will not be badly damaged by a cat's rambunctiousness.

The leaves are a treat for your cat and can be given to him fresh or dried. A tea is also made from the leaves that is said to be relaxing and soothing.

CHAMOMILE (*Anthemis nobilis*)

Plant: perennial, hardy to —20°

Height: 3-12 inches

Soil: moist, well drained

Exposure: sun, semi-shade

Propagation: seeds, divisions

Uses: tea, ground cover

There are several species of Anthemis, but *A. nobilis,* called Roman or English chamomile, is the one used most often in herb gardens. It is perennial and evergreen, growing in a soft-textured mat 3 inches high when not blooming but rising to 12 inches high when the flowers are allowed to develop. Its aromatic leaves are a light, bright green and finely cut, resembling fingers on a hand. The summer-blooming flowers have white daisy-like rays and yellow centers. Chamomile is a creeping herb and the

stems root themselves as they spread. When mowed, chamomile makes a good lawn substitute.

Roman chamomile, or ground apple, has always had an important part in herb gardens. When bruised or walked on, it emits a delightful fragrance; Shakespeare's Falstaff says of it, "the more it is trodden on the faster it grows," and it has been a traditional ground cover over garden paths and walks. Old-fashioned garden seats of earth also were covered with chamomile. A popular belief held that chamomile was the garden's doctor and when planted near sick or dying plants it would cure them. The flowers are used to flavor a dry Spanish sherry, and a tea brewed from the flowers has been taken for nervousness.

Chamomile grows best in sun or semi-shade and moist, light, well drained soil. It does not seem to last long in dry summer areas, and brass buttons (*Cotula squalida*) is often substituted for it there. Sow seeds in the early spring or late fall. Once plants are established they will spread by runners and can be divided for additional plantings.

A tea may be brewed from chamomile blossoms, and they are also used in a hair rinse preparation.

CHERVIL (*Anthriscus cerefolium*)

Plant: annual

Height: 1-2 feet

Soil: average, moist

Exposure: partial shade

Propagation: seeds

Uses: culinary

Chervil is an annual with curly and very finely cut and divided leaves like parsley, growing on stems 1-2 feet tall. They smell and taste mildly of anise. Clusters of white flowers grow in umbrellalike clusters at the tops of the flowering stems.

This herb and sweet cicely (*Myrrhis odorata*, page 75) —which is also known as sweet or giant chervil but is a perennial—are often confused with one another, and when many early writers speak of chervil they are referring to sweet cicely. Chervil was once highly valued as a salad herb, and during the Middle Ages the roots were eaten during plagues with the curious stipulation that they be washed but never scraped or pared. The leaves were also dried and applied to bruises in a compress.

Chervil is grown from seeds in good, slightly moist garden soil and in partial shade. Flower stems are often cut before they bloom to encourage fuller foliage which is harvested in mid or late summer. If you allow flowers to mature, chervil will reseed itself readily.

Although chervil often is considered a gourmet parsley, it has a more pronounced, slightly anise-like flavor. When used with other herbs it enhances their flavor. The fresh leaves also can be added to salads.

CHIVES (*Allium schoenoprasum*)

Plant: perennial, hardy to —35°

Height: to 2 feet

Soil: moist, fairly rich

Exposure: sun, partial shade

Propagation: seeds, divisions

Uses: culinary

The round, hollow leaves with an oniony flavor grow from small bulbs in grass-like clumps. Chives can grow up to 2 feet tall but are usually shorter because the tops of the leaves are continually being clipped for use as a seasoning. The clover-like flowers are a rose-purple color and appear first as a little bulblike bud among the round green leaves. The plant is pretty enough to use as an edging for flower borders or an herb garden, and the flowers even can be cut and used in arrangements.

Another allium species similar to common chives is garlic chives or Chinese chives (*A. tuberosum*). They resemble common chives in their clumping growth form, but the leaves are flat instead of round and are a powdery gray color. The flowers of garlic chives grow in clusters above the tips of the leaves and are white. Leaves have a mild garlic flavor.

Chives do best in moist, fairly rich soil and in full sun. Common chives are evergreen (or nearly so) in mild regions, and go dormant where winters are severe. Chinese chives are less vigorous than common chives and more inclined to winter dormancy. They both require the same culture.

Bring clumps of common and Chinese chives indoors in containers for the winter to assure a supply of fresh leaves for cooking.

Chives are usually bought as small plants, but they also can be grown from seeds. If you have a clump of chives, you can increase it easily by dividing the roots.

Use chopped chives in salads, cheese and egg dishes,

gravies, and soups for a delicate onion or garlic flavor. Cut the tops of the leaves as soon as the plants are established. They usually are used fresh but can be preserved by drying or freezing.

CORIANDER (*Coriandrum sativum*)

Plant: annual

Height: 12-18 inches

Soil: light, moderately rich

Exposure: sun

Propagation: seeds

Uses: culinary

Coriander is the name under which you will find seeds of this plant sold, but if you encounter fresh leaves for sale in the market they probably will be called Chinese parsley or cilantro. Coriander is a parsley relative and looks something like it but is an annual. It has one central flowering stem that grows upright from a tap root to a height of 12-18 inches with other flowering stems branching out from it. The leaves growing on the main stem are oval with toothed edges, but those on the side branches are more lacy and delicate, resembling anise or dill. The small pinkish-white flowers are in flat, umbrellalike clusters at the ends of the stems.

Coriander is an ancient herb and referred to in the Bible in a comparison to Manna. Its seeds have been found in Egyptian tombs, and the Romans used them to preserve meat. Although the seeds have long been used to season foods, one herbalist in the 16th century had an odd belief that using too many (or green) seeds would cause a distressed and troubled mind.

Another sun lover, coriander prefers moderately rich soil that is light and drains well; but plant it in partial shade where summers are hot. It can easily be grown from seeds—sown where the plants are to grow—in the early spring. If you want to grow it primarily for the fresh leaves you can easily plant it in containers (indoors or outside) and harvest plants when they reach about 6 inches. By sowing new seeds every two weeks or so you can have a continuous crop. Otherwise, you can pick young, tender leaves a few at a time beginning when plants reach 4-6 inches; this will work for a few months until plants either wear out, become tough, or bloom.

The mature seeds are pleasingly aromatic and flavorful; use them in potpourris and to flavor beans, stews, sausage, pastries, and some wines. Harvest seeds in mid-summer as soon as they are ripe, or their weight will bend the stems to the ground and the seeds will drop off.

Fresh leaves often are an ingredient of Mediterranean, Latin American, Far Eastern, and some Oriental foods. Its sharp, distinctive flavor (herb writers in the past often warned readers about the strong, unpleasant flavor of the leaves) combines best with fowl, meats, and spicy seasonings and sauces.

COSTMARY (*Chrysanthemum balsamita*)

Plant: perennial, hardy to —20°

Height: 2-4 feet

Soil: average, well drained

Exposure: sun, partial shade

Propagation: divisions

Uses: tea, fragrance

Costmary is another perennial member of the large chrysanthemum clan. Leaves are large—to about 7 inches long—and have toothed edges; flower stems are erect and stiff, and grow 2-4 feet tall. Plants that have flowers without petals are *C. b.* variety *tanacetoides*. Although its appearance is somewhat weedy, the sweet scent of the foliage makes it a pleasant herb for the garden. If the leggy stems are cut back, the fragrant, gray-green clumps of leaves make a good looking edging for other plants.

Costmary (or alecost, as it has been called in the past) has always been valued for its fragrance and flavor. The leaves were once used in brewing beer and ale, in sausage making, and in salads. It was also used to make a sweet water for washing. In many European countries costmary is dedicated to the Virgin Mary, but it also has associations with St. Mary Magdalene and is known as "Sweet Mary." Early American colonists used the leaves as a bookmarker in their Bibles, bringing about another common name, Bible leaf.

Give costmary a good, well drained garden soil and full sun or sun-filtered shade. It dies to the ground in cold winter climates but will return in the spring. Grow new plants from divisions taken in the spring or fall.

The minty flavored leaves can be used as a garnish in iced drinks or can be brewed into a tea. If used very sparingly, the young tips are good for seasoning a simple green salad. Leaves are frequently placed in drawers and closets to give linens a pleasant aroma.

DILL (*Anethum graveolens*)

Plant: annual

Height: 3-4 feet

Soil: average, well drained

Exposure: sun

Propagation: seeds

Uses: culinary

Dill has finely cut, feathery, light green leaves similar to fennel but shorter and smaller. Each plant is a single stem which reaches 3-4 feet at maturity—about 2 months after the seeds are sown. Small, greenish yellow flowers grow in umbrellalike heads that are about 6 inches across. In early fall the flowers go to seed and will readily self sow if not harvested. Both leaves and seeds are aromatic.

Dill was a favorite herb of magicians and sorcerers who used it to help cast their spells. But another ancient folk belief was that branches of dill hung above the door would protect a home from witchcraft. One herbalist recommended boiling dill in wine and then smelling the fumes to cure hiccoughs.

Give dill full sun and well drained, good garden soil. Propagate by seeds sown in the spring, or by allowing plants to self sow in the fall. Dill has a tap root and does not transplant easily.

The seeds and leaves of dill have a sharp, slightly bitter taste that is reminiscent of caraway. Both are used in preparing fish, chicken, lamb, stews, sauces, salad dressings, and breads. Harvest the seeds when they ripen but before they drop to the ground. Use the leaves fresh or dried, but for the greatest flavor pick them just as the flowers are opening.

DITTANY OF CRETE (*Amaracus dictamnus*)

Plant: perennial, hardy to 15°

Height: 1 foot

Soil: average, well drained

Exposure: sun

Propagation: seeds, cuttings

Uses: culinary, ground cover

With its soft, round, downy leaves and minutely detailed flowers, dittany is a highly ornamental plant. Its slender, arching stems, each about a foot long, have opposite pairs of thick rounded leaves that look somewhat like beads on a string. Leaves are only ½-¾ inch long and are covered with a white, woolly hair. The tiny, rather inconspicuous flowers are pink to purplish in color and grow at the ends of the stems from summer through fall. The hop-like flower bracts hold on for a long time in the fall and are the most ornamental part.

Dittany used to be very highly regarded as a cure for wounds. Venus was supposed to have given the plant to Aeneas during the Trojan Wars to cure his soldiers, and afterwards people said that it was able to remove iron and splinters from any wound and cure it immediately.

Full sun, ordinary well drained garden soil, and routine watering are satisfactory for dittany. It can be propagated from seeds, cuttings, or root division. This is an especially attractive plant for hanging containers where it will drape over the sides. It must be brought indoors during cold winters.

As a culinary herb, dittany can be used in most of the same foods as marjoram and oregano.

FEVERFEW
(*Chrysanthemum parthenium*)

Plant: perennial, hardy to —20°

Height: 1-3 feet

Soil: well drained, moist

Exposure: sun, partial shade

Propagation: cuttings, division

Uses: landscape only

Feverfew is a compact, rugged perennial chrysanthemum with very divided and cut leaves that have a pungent aroma which some people find unpleasant. The species has single white flowers which produce quantities of seed that germinate readily; in some areas it has a reputation as a weed. The plants grow between 1 and 3 feet tall, depending on the variety. 'Golden Ball' has bright yellow flower heads and no rays. 'Silver Ball' is completely double with only the white rays showing. 'Aureum,' commonly sold in flats as 'Golden Feather,' features chartreuse colored foliage as its principal attraction.

As the name implies, feverfew was once used in treating fevers. A tea brewed from the leaves and wreaths

of its foliage placed about the head were two folk remedies for a headache.

Growth is easy in a moist, well drained soil and sun or partial shade. Plants grown from seeds sown in the spring will produce bloom by midsummer. Thereafter, propagate by dividing established plants in the spring or fall, or by cuttings taken from the base of stems, or—for the species —by simply transplanting volunteer seedlings.

This herb is valued as an ornamental in perennial borders and for its cut flowers which can be used in arrangements.

FENNEL (*Foeniculum* species)

Plant: perennial

Height: to 5 feet

Soil: light, well drained

Exposure: sun

Propagation: seeds

Uses: culinary

There are several species of fennel. Common fennel (*F. vulgare*) is a perennial that usually is cultivated as an annual. Its upright, hollow, fleshy stems grow to about 5 feet tall, with thin, straight, and very finely cut leaves. Flat clusters of yellow flowers grow at the ends of the stems above the foliage. Fennel looks very much like dill but is taller and more coarse. A red form is often grown for its colored foliage.

A variety of the species is Florence fennel (*F. v. dulche*) which is lower growing than common fennel with larger and thicker leaf bases. It is cultivated for its thick, bulblike base which is usually harvested before flowers appear and eaten as a vegetable called Finocchio. Blanch the base of the stem or "bulb" by piling dirt around it when it has become the size of an egg; after about 10 days it will be ready for harvesting.

To many people, fennel is a familiar plant from vacant lots and fields where it often grows wild. In the past, fennel was highly valued as a supposed cure for eye disorders and blindness. It was also commonly eaten to prevent overweight and cure fatness, perhaps in a belief that the thin leaves would bestow their characteristics on the consumer.

Common fennel prefers full sun, and light, well drained good garden soil. Propagate by seeds sown in the spring where the plants are to grow. Seeds of Florence fennel can also be sown in the late summer for a fall crop of leaves and stalks; thin seedlings to about one foot apart.

Both leaves and seeds of fennel have a pleasant anise or licorice flavor and are a good seasoning for fish, cheeses, vegetables, and some pastries. The stems, particularly the fleshy base of Florence fennel, may be harvested while still tender—just before the flowers blossom—and eaten raw or cooked as a vegetable. Harvest the leaves just as the flowers are beginning to bloom; they are best pre-served by freezing. The seeds can be dried.

GARLIC (*Allium sativum*)

Plant: perennial bulb

Height: 2-3 feet

Soil: rich, well drained

Exposure: sun

Propagation: division

Uses: culinary

The distinctive flavor and aroma of garlic is familiar to many people, for it is one of the most frequently used culinary herbs. Plants are bulbous perennials that grow about 2-3 feet high and die back to the bulb each year after flowering. The bases of its long, flat, narrow leaves sheath the flower stalk which grows up to produce a small cluster of white flowers at the top. Each individual bulb multiplies, as the plant matures during the growing season, into a cluster of bulblets (called "cloves") that are held together by a pinkish-white, paperlike skin. These bulbs are then dug up for use and replanting.

Garlic and its other relatives in the onion clan are among the oldest known foods and seasonings. Garlic is traditionally thought to be a strength giving herb. It was eaten extensively by Egyptians working on the pyramids and by Greek and Roman athletes while training and before contests.

Grow garlic from mother bulbs or sets which are sold at many nurseries and seed stores. Break these bulbs up into individual bulblets (cloves) and plant them base downward 1-2 inches deep. Plants thrive best in rich, well drained soil. In mild winter areas plant the bulbs in October to December for an early summer harvest. Where winters are severe, plant early in the spring.

Harvest garlic bulbs by digging or pulling them up when the leafy tops of the stems begin to droop over toward the ground. Dry the whole bulbs in a dry, airy room; then remove the tops and roots and store in a cool place.

Garlic is such a versatile seasoning that it can be used in just about any dish—and particularly with meats, stews, chicken, salads, and sauces.

GERANIUMS (*Pelargonium* species)

Plant: perennial, hardy to 20°

Height: to 4 feet

Soil: average, well drained

Exposure: sun, partial shade

Propagation: cuttings, seeds

Uses: fragrance, culinary

Of the many different kinds of geraniums, those that are best suited for the herb garden are the scented-leafed species and varieties. Most of these have small flowers in clusters and interestingly textured leaves that release a distinctive fragrance when pinched or bruised.

Rose geranium (*P. graveolens*) has slightly hairy, deep green, lobed leaves, with each of the 5-7 lobes again divided and toothed. Their fragrance is pungent, spicy, and somewhat rose-like. The leaves are used frequently in making potpourri, jelly, and custards. Flowers appear in clusters of 5-10 and are rose colored or purple with pink veins, but generally they are not showy.

Lemon-scented geranium (*P. crispum*) has small, crinkly leaves which can be floated in finger bowls, used in pot-pourris, or dried in bunches and hung in closets to give clothes and linens a fresh, lemony scent. The plant grows to about 2-3 feet high and has small lavender flowers. Orange geranium ('Prince of Orange') has larger and broader leaves than the lemon species. It is shrubby and has white flowers with a black spot on the upper petals. *P. crispum* 'Variegatum' is peach-scented and has small crinkled leaves mottled with yellow. The flowers are lavender.

Lime-scented geranium (*P. nervosum*) grows into a bushy plant with round, somewhat ruffled, light green leaves that have toothed margins. Their lavender flowers are abundant and showy.

Nutmeg geranium (*P. fragrans*) is a branching, rather bushy plant with small, roundish, gray-green leaves. It bears small white flowers with pink veins.

Apple-scented geranium (*P. odoratissimum*) has trailing stems up to 1½ feet long that are clothed with roundish, ruffled leaves. White flowers grow in fluffy clusters.

Peppermint geranium (P. *tomentosum*) has large—3-5 inches wide—attractively lobed leaves. The plants are rather tender but will spread to 5 or 6 feet in warm climates. Small white flowers appear in fluffy clusters. This variety makes a good hanging basket plant.

Almond-scented geranium 'Pretty Polly' has attractive, light green foliage and large silvery pink flowers with dark crimson spots.

An apricot-smelling variety (P. *scabrum* 'M. Ninon') is a large shrub with shiny, dark green leaves and showy carmine red flowers with darker markings.

Coconut-scented geranium (P. *grossularioides*) is a low growing, trailing plant with dark green, rounded leaves. It bears clusters of tiny, rosy red flowers.

Filbert-scented geranium ('Schottesham Pet') makes a low (1-foot-high) mounding plant with deeply cut, light green foliage and red flowers.

Geraniums are tender, so in cold winter areas grow them in pots or boxes and bring them indoors during the winter. They thrive indoors and may even bloom if placed in a window that will provide enough sunlight. In mild winter areas, grow them outdoors all year in permanent garden plantings or in containers. Use the sprawling kinds as a ground cover around trees or plant them in hanging containers.

In coastal areas plant geraniums in full sun, but where summers are hot and dry they will do best in partial shade. Give them good, well drained garden soil and keep it somewhat on the dry side (but don't let them dry out completely). As a rule, geraniums planted in the garden need little fertilizing unless your soil is sandy or very well drained. Then, they may need 2-3 applications each year of a complete fertilizer. Pale foliage or lack of new growth also indicate a need for fertilizer. Pinch growing tips in the early stages to encourage side branching, and remove flowers as they begin to fade to encourage more bloom. You can start new plants from seeds or stem cuttings.

The germanders are very rugged, small to medium-sized shrubs that will thrive in heat and poor soil.

Teucrium chamaedrys is low-growing with many upright stems 1-2 feet high. The dark green leaves are about ¾ inch long with toothed margins and cover the branches densely. Reddish purple or white, ¾-inch flowers appear in loose spikes during the summer. This species makes a good edging or low clipped hedge. To keep the growth looking neat, shear back once or twice a year to force side branching. T. c. 'Prostratum' has flowers and foliage that are similar to T. *chamaedrys* but it is much more prostrate, growing only 4-6 inches high and spreading to about 3 feet. Plants spread by underground runners and can be invasive. For a ground cover, set plants 2 feet apart.

T. *fruticans*, or bush germander, is a loose, silvery-stemmed shrub growing 4-8 feet high and about 9 feet wide. The leaves are 1¼ inches long, gray green above and silvery white below, giving the plant an overall silvery white effect. Lavender-blue, ¾-inch-long flowers grow in spikes at the ends of the branches during most of the year in warm climates; they are attractive but not showy.

Germander often was used in knot gardens as a border hedge along paths and planting beds. Medicinally it once was a major ingredient in a blend of herbs used for curing gout, and was supposed to be a good herb to take for strengthening the brain and thinking.

Germanders are good plants for sun and heat, and endure poor, rocky soils well. They must have good drainage, however, as prolonged wet soil is fatal.

Germander's principal use today is in the landscape as a low hedge or ground cover.

GERMANDER (*Teucrium* species)

Plant: perennial, hardy to 0°

Height: to 2 feet or to 8 feet

Soil: poor, well drained

Exposure: sun

Propagation: cuttings

Uses: landscape only

HOREHOUND (*Marrubium vulgare*)

Plant: perennial, hardy to —30°

Height: 1-3 feet

Soil: poor, dry, well drained

Exposure: sun

Propagation: seeds, division

Uses: culinary

This is a perennial relative of mint with much-branched stems that grow about 2 feet high. Its aromatic, wrinkled, gray-green leaves are covered with downy white hair; flowers also are white. As a garden ornamental it sometimes looks rather weedy, but it can serve as an edging in a gray garden.

Horehound is an age-old medication for coughs and sore throats. The ancient Greeks and Romans used it as an antidote for poisoning, to cure insect and snake bites, and to keep scorpions and spiders away from their homes. It has become naturalized and a weed in parts of California.

It grows easily in poor, sandy, dry soil and full sun; once established, it can be rather aggressive. Sow seeds in flats and transplant the seedlings into the garden 12 inches apart.

Horehound is used to make horehound candy, and a tea brewed from the leaves is sometimes taken to relieve a cough or cold.

HYSSOP (*Hyssopus officinalis*)

Plant: perennial, hardy to —35°

Height: 1½-2 feet

Soil: well drained, alkaline

Exposure: sun

Propagation: cuttings, division

Uses: landscape only

Hyssop is a compact, shrubby perennial that grows between 18-24 inches high. Its smooth, narrow leaves taper to a point at the end and grow opposite one another on the woody stems. Their color is dark, glossy green and they have a pungent aroma and resinous taste. The small flowers are white, pink, or blue, depending on the variety, and appear profusely between July and November in spikes at the ends of stems.

There are a number of references to a hyssop in the Bible. It is mentioned as a purification for lepers, and David prayed that he would be purged and cleansed by it. Jesus Christ was supposed to have been given a sponge dipped in vinegar and hyssop during his crucifixion. This hyssop, however, may not have been the hyssop we are familiar with today but a variety of marjoram or savory instead. Branches of hyssop were once thought to protect against "the evil eye," and wives would hang bunches of them in their homes to avert this curse.

Grow hyssop in full sun and light, well drained soil that is slightly alkaline. New plants may be grown from seeds sown in moist soil in the spring. Once established, hyssop will reseed itself; or, you can propagate it from root divisions and stem cuttings. If it is kept clipped, hyssop will make a good low hedge.

The flavor of hyssop is not pleasant to many modern tastes, but you can try the leaves in stews or brew a tea from them. They also make an interesting seasoning for rich or fatty fish. The flowers are attractive in fresh arrangements.

LAVENDER (*Lavandula* species)

Plant: perennial, hardy to 0° (except *L. dentata*, to 15°)

Height: 1½-4 feet

Soil: dry, well drained

Exposure: sun

Propagation: seeds, cuttings

Uses: fragrance

One of the most traditional herb garden plants is lavender, and the most widely planted and used species is English lavender (*L. spica*). The woody, upright stems grow 3-4 feet high, and each plant spreads to about 3 feet across. Leaves are gray and narrow, about 2 inches long with smooth margins. Lavender colored flowers grow on 24-inch-long spikes at the ends of the stems in July and August. There are several dwarf varieties of *L. spica*. 'Compacta' is 8 inches tall, 12-15 inches wide, with deep purple flowers. 'Munstead' is a popular dwarf, 18 inches tall with deep lavender-blue flowers. 'Hidcote' grows slowly to about 1 foot and has purple flowers. 'Twickel Purple,' 2-3 feet high, has fan-like clusters of purple flowers on extra long stalks.

French lavender (*L. dentata*) reaches about 3 feet high and has bright green, 1-1½ inch leaves with square toothed edges. Lavender-purple flowers grow in short, blunt clusters, each topped with a tuft of petal-like bracts. In mild winter climates it blooms almost continually. There is also a gray-leafed variety: *L. d. candicans*.

Spanish lavender (*L. stoechas*) is a 1½-3-foot-tall, stocky plant with short and narrow gray leaves. The flowers are dark purple and about ⅛ inch long growing in dense, short flower spikes topped with a tuft of large purple petal-like bracts. They bloom in the early summer.

Spike lavender (*L. latifolia*) looks much like English lavender but has broader leaves and flower stalks that often are branched.

Lavender has always been highly prized for the fragrance of its blossoms. They have been used to perfume soaps, pillows, bath and toilet waters, and even the stuffings of chairs. Medicinally, lavender was used to revive a person from a faint or swoon.

All the lavenders need sun and loose, fast draining soil. Prune immediately after blooming to keep plants compact and neat. Grow from small plants bought at the nursery, seeds sown in flats, or from stem cuttings with a heel on the end.

Use the flowers for their fragrance in potpourris, sachets, perfumed baths, and flower arrangements. Harvest when they are in full bloom. The plants are often grown as an edging or hedge in the garden (pages 27-29).

LEMON BALM (*Melissa officinalis*)

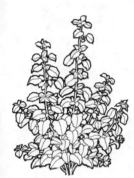

Plant: perennial, hardy to —20°

Height: 2 feet

Soil: moist, rich

Exposure: sun, partial shade

Propagation: cuttings, division

Uses: culinary, fragrance

Lemon balm (or sweet balm, as it is sometimes called) is a lemony scented and flavored, much-branched perennial that grows to about 2 feet high. The light green leaves are heavily veined, 2-3 inches long, and have scalloped margins. White flowers grow along the stems throughout the summer but they are not numerous or conspicuous.

Beekeepers valued lemon balm because it was supposed to attract bees; it was also believed that bees would stay together and in the garden longer if their hives were rubbed with the leaves. Lemon balm also was a popular strewing herb, and chairs used to be rubbed with the foliage to give them a pleasant lemon scent. A tea made from its leaves was reputed to dispel melancholy and sadness, while a compress of leaves was applied to scorpion stings and mad-dog bites.

Lemon balm will thrive in rich, moist soil and in sun or partial shade. It is very hardy and spreads so rapidly that it can become invasive. Shear plants back occasionally to keep growth compact and contained. The seeds take a long time to germinate and should be sown in the fall for spring plants. You can propagate lemon balm from root divisions or stem cuttings.

Use the fresh or dried leaves to make a refreshing lemon flavored tea, float them in claret cups and punches, or add to fruit salads for a subtle lemon flavor. They are also an ingredient in many potpourris and produce a fragrant oil used in perfume manufacture.

LEMON VERBENA (*Aloysia triphylla*)

Plant: perennial, hardy to 10°

Height: 6 feet

Soil: average, well drained

Exposure: sun

Propagation: cuttings

Uses: culinary, fragrance

This deciduous herb-shrub has very branching, woody stems that grow to about 6 feet high. Legginess is its natural growth form, although by pinch-pruning you can shape it into an interesting tracery against a wall. The simplest solution, however, is to let it grow naturally out of lower plants that will conceal the branchiness. Its narrow, 3-inch leaves are arranged in whorls of 3 or 4 along the branches. Very small, white or lilac flowers are carried in spikes at the ends of the stems.

Lemon verbena is a native of Central and South America and was probably brought to North America and Europe by Spanish explorers.

Plant lemon verbena where it will have full sun, in any good, well drained garden soil. It can be grown from seeds but they usually take a long time to germinate; much easier is to start new plants from stem cuttings. Although hardy in warm winter areas, it must be brought indoors before frosts in harsher climates.

The leaves often are included in potpourri, to which they add a lemony fragrance. They also can be brewed into a tea or used like mint as a garnish in iced drinks. Place a leaf in the bottom of a jar of homemade apple jelly for a spritely hint of lemon. Sprigs placed in drawers among linens will give them a lemony scent.

LOVAGE (*Levisticum officinale*)

Plant: perennial, hardy to —5°

Height: 4-6 feet

Soil: moist, slightly alkaline

Exposure: sun, partial shade

Propagation: seeds

Uses: culinary

This perennial is celery-like in all respects except size: The thick, coarse clumps may reach 4-6 feet tall. Leaves are deep glossy green and are very finely divided and cut, while flowers grow in flat-topped clusters above the foliage. The stalks, seeds, and foliage taste and smell like celery.

Native to southern Europe, particularly the Mediterranean countries, lovage probably was brought to Great Britain by the Romans. It now grows wild in a few parts of northern Europe, England, and Scotland. Lovage was a component of the most ancient herb gardens, and the leaves are one of the oldest salad greens; the stems have been eaten as a vegetable, and the seeds candied as a confection. Herbalists of the 16th century recommended taking lovage for coughs and stomach disorders.

The plant prefers a moist, slightly alkaline, and fairly rich soil well supplied with organic matter. Growth is best in sun or partial shade. Indoors, lovage will survive without direct sun as long as it receives good light. Start from seeds sown in the garden in the late fall to produce seedlings the following spring. You also can sow seeds in containers in the winter and transplant young seedlings into the garden in the spring.

Harvest the leaves when they are young and tender, and use them fresh or dried in soups, stews, and salads. The seeds can be used crushed or whole in the same way. Blanch the stems and eat them like celery or slice them into salads, stews, and soups.

Marjoram is a Mediterranean herb and may not have reached Great Britain until the 10th or 11th century where it was highly valued for the pleasing aroma of its leaves. There are several stories and folk customs surrounding it. The goddess Venus was supposed to have created marjoram and been the first to grow it; the sweet smell and flavor of its leaves are said to have come from her touch. It was believed by the Greeks that marjoram growing on a tomb or grave was a sign that the deceased's soul was contented. Wreaths made from the stems of marjoram were placed on the heads of a bridal couple in ancient Greece and Rome. Marjoram was also one of the fragrant strewing herbs placed on floors to sweeten the air as it was walked on. The dried leaves were used in sweet bags placed among linens, and a tea was made from them that was taken to relieve colds and congestion.

Marjoram should be grown in full sun and a moist, slightly alkaline soil. Sow seeds early in the spring. You also can propagate marjoram from stem cuttings or root divisions. To prevent the stems from growing too woody, keep the blossoms cut off and the plant trimmed. It makes an attractive container plant and can easily be raised indoors if given enough sun.

Marjoram leaves are a popular seasoning in a number of foods. Add fresh or dried leaves to meats, salads, vinegars, and casseroles. They also can be used to make teas and jellies.

MARJORAM (*Majorana hortensis*)

Plant: perennial

Height: 1-2 feet

Soil: alkaline, moist

Exposure: sun

Propagation: seeds, cuttings

Uses: culinary

A tender perennial, sweet marjoram is sometimes grown as an annual or indoors in containers in harsh winter climates. It has semi-woody stems that branch upwards from the base to about 1-2 feet. The leaves are small and oval—light green on the top and a gray-green color on the underside. Small whitish flowers grow from knot-like clusters of tiny leaves growing close together at the tips of the stems. These "knots" have four sides and appear singly or in groups of 2 or more.

MINTS (*Mentha* species)

Plant: perennial, hardy to —20°
(M. pulegium, M. *requinii* to 5°)

Height: 1-3 feet

Soil: moist, rich

Exposure: shade

Propagation: cuttings, division

Uses: culinary, fragrance

From the large assortment of mint species and varieties there are many that you can grow. Typically, these plants have square stems and opposite leaves that are aromatic when crushed. The seven that are described here are among the most important and most frequently grown.

Orange mint or bergamot mint (M. *citrata*) grows to about 2 feet high and has broad, dark green, 2-inch leaves that are edged with purple. They taste and smell slightly of oranges, combined with the characteristic minty aroma. The blossoms are lavender and grow in dense flower spikes during midsummer. The stems of this species are reddish purple and nearly round.

Golden apple mint (*M. gentilis*) has smooth, deep green leaves variegated with yellow. The plant grows to about 2 feet and makes an attractive ground cover where taller spring-flowering bulbs are planted.

Peppermint (*M. piperita*)—or its flavor—is familiar to many people. The plant grows to 3 feet high and has strongly scented, 3-inch leaves with toothed edges. Small purple flowers appear in 1-3-inch-long spikes at the ends of stems.

Pennyroyal (*M. pulegium*) is another attractive mint, but it should not be confused with American mock pennyroyal (*Hedeoma pulegiodes*) which is not a mint at all. It is prostrate and branching with downy, oval leaves that are no more than ½-inch long. Small, rosy lilac flowers bloom late in the summer and early autumn. It is a less hardy, and far less neat, ground cover than Corsican mint but—in its favor—it is said to repel insects from the garden.

Jewel mint of Corsica or Corsican mint (*M. requienii*) is a creeping sort that rarely grows over 1 inch high. It has tiny, round, bright green leaves that form a moss-like mat. In summer, small, light purple flowers appear. The foliage has a delightful minty or sagelike fragrance when bruised or crushed under foot.

Apple mint (*M. rotundifolia*) has stiff stems that grow 20 to 30 inches high. The rounded leaves are slightly hairy and gray-green, about 1-4 inches long. The purplish white flowers are produced in 2-3 inch spikes.

Spearmint (*M. spicata*) is another of the most familiar species and is the one used commonly with roast lamb and in mint jelly. Its dark green leaves are slightly smaller than those of peppermint and look and feel crinkly. The stems will grow 1½-2 feet high if not pinched back.

The ancient Greeks believed that when Pluto, god of the underworld, became enraptured by the beauty of Menthe (a young nymph), his wife Prosperpine turned her into this herb and left her forever to grow in the shadows and moisture. However, Menthe was still loved by the Greeks and has continued to find friends ever since. Mints have been used in innumerable ways in the past. The ancient Pharisees of Biblical times paid their taxes with its leaves. Ancient medicine has recommended using the leaves for bites of mad dogs, to prevent indigestion, to cure mouth and gum ailments, in a preparation for ulcers, to heal skin diseases, and to stimulate the appetite. One old herbalist warns, however, that if a wounded man eats it, his injuries will never heal, while another claims that it must never be cut or harvested with shears or a blade made of iron. Previous writers are not always explicit as to which species of mint they are talking about, but the distinct flavor and aroma that most of the species share to some degree makes it clear that this is what made them so highly favored.

Modern commerce makes many uses of mints. Spearmint and peppermint are two of the most common flavorings for everything from chewing gum to mouthwashes and medicines.

Most mints will grow almost anywhere except in hot, direct sun. They do best, however, in a light, moderately rich soil that is moist and in shade or partial shade. These herbs spread rapidly by underground stems and runners and can be propagated very simply by layering, division, or stem cuttings. Their invasive nature can be contained by planting in pots or boxes, or sinking header boards 6-8 inches into the ground around their roots. Keep flowers pinched back to encourage bushy growth.

Use the leaves fresh or dried in any number of different ways: add them to potpourris, lamb, and jelly; spearmint is the best for garnishing iced drinks; fresh leaves of peppermint, pineapple, apple, and orange mints can be added to fruit cocktails or sprinkled over ice cream.

NASTURTIUM (*Tropaeolum* species)

Plant: perennial grown as annual

Height: 15 inches

Soil: sandy, moist

Exposure: sun

Propagation: seeds

Uses: culinary

Nasturtiums are native to Central and South America and grow wild in some of the sandy California beach areas. There are two species which are most often grown in herb gardens. *T. majus* has long stems that will trail over the ground or climb to 6 feet by coiling its leaf stalks around an upright support. *T. minus* is more dwarfed and compact, growing to about 15 inches. Both of these species have round, shield-shaped, bright green leaves growing on long stalks which are attached to the center of the leaves. The flowers are broad and shaped like a horn with a long spur at one end and opening out into a bell shape at the other. Their colors range from maroon, red-brown, orange, yellow, and red, to creamy white. There are both single and double flowered forms. Nasturtiums have a distinctive appearance, and though perennial they are most often treated as annuals.

Nasturtiums are easy to grow in most soils that have good drainage, but they really thrive in soil that is sandy and exposed to the sun for a good part of the day. Sow seeds in the early spring when there is no danger of frost. They grow and bloom quickly and will often reseed themselves.

The climbing and trailing kinds will cover fences, banks, stumps, and rocks. Use dwarf species for bedding, to cover fading bulb foliage, and generally quick flower color. They also make good container specimens and house plants.

Nasturtium leaves and flowers have a peppery flavor like watercress and are often used in salads. The unripened seed pods can be pickled and used as a substitute for capers.

OREGANO (*Origanum vulgare*)

Plant: perennial, hardy to —30°

Height: 2-2½ feet

Soil: average, well drained

Exposure: sun

Propagation: seeds, cuttings

Uses: culinary

Oregano—also known as wild marjoram—is closely related to sweet marjoram. It also is a perennial and grows to about 2-2½ feet. The leaves are rounded and come to a blunt point at the tip, but often are larger and coarser than those of sweet marjoram and have a darker green color. Small, purplish pink blossoms grow at the ends of the stems. Oregano is shrubby and tends to spread by invasive underground stems.

There is a legend that describes the origin of oregano. A young servant to Cinyras, the king of Cyprus, was carrying a large vessel, full of valuable perfume which the king was particularly fond of. Accidentally, he dropped the container, spilling its contents. He was so afraid of what his punishment would be that he fainted, and, while lying unconscious on the ground where the oil had spilled, he was metamorphosed into the oregano plant.

Oregano grows in well drained, good garden soil where plants receive full sun. It requires routine watering. Like sweet marjoram, the flowers should be kept cut back to encourage bushiness and thick foliage. It makes a good container plant but should be replaced about every 3 years when it becomes woody. Grow new plants from seeds or by dividing an established plant.

The leaves have a sharper flavor than sweet marjoram and taste a little of thyme. Use them fresh or dried in the same foods you would marjoram or thyme, especially Italian and Spanish or Mexican dishes.

PARSLEY (*Petroselinum crispum*)

Plant: biennial

Height: 6-12 inches

Soil: moist, moderately rich

Exposure: shade, partial sun

Propagation: seeds

Uses: culinary

There are several species of parsley, but the curly French parsley (*Petroselinum crispum*) is the most popular in the garden because of its decorative foliage. The leaves are tufted and finely cut with serrated or toothed edges and wrinkled surfaces. Italian, or plain-leafed, parsley (*P. c. var. filicinum*) is more favored by many cooks because it has more flavor than French parsley, but the latter reigns supreme as a garnish for many different foods. The 6-12-inch plants are biennial—flowering in their second year—but most gardeners treat them as annuals, starting anew from seeds each year.

There are several folk legends about parsley. One says that it is unlucky to transplant parsley from an old garden into a new one. Another tells that the seeds must go to the devil and back again 9 times before they sprout—an attempt to explain the slowness with which the seeds germinate. Some gardeners believed that someone in a house that parsley was planted near would die shortly afterwards. Parsley was used quite frequently by the ancient Greeks. Garlands or bouquets of the leaves were hung about the neck or worn as a crown at banquets to absorb the fumes of wine and prevent drunkenness. After eating, parsley was chewed to clean the mouth and sweeten one's breath. Parsley was also made into wreaths that crowned the winners at Nemean Games. Occasionally, it was used as a strewing herb.

Grow parsley in sun-filtered shade or morning sun and afternoon shade, and in partially moist soil that is moderately rich. Buy small plants of parsley from the nursery, or sow seeds where they are to grow in April if you live in a cold winter climate and in December through May if your winters are mild. Soak the seeds in warm water for 24 hours before planting as they usually take several weeks to sprout. Thin seedlings 6-8 inches apart. This herb is a favorite so you will probably want a quantity of plants.

Parsley is used fresh as a garnish, and fresh or dried in many different foods such as vegetables, meats, stews, casseroles, salads, soups, and eggs. Harvest the leaves before plants flower: Once the flower spikes form, the leaves become bitter tasting.

ROSEMARY (*Rosmarinus officinalis*)

Plant: perennial, hardy to 0°

Height: 2-6 feet

Soil: dry, poor, well drained

Exposure: sun

Propagation: seeds, cuttings

Uses: culinary

Where winters are mild enough, rosemary is an outstanding shrubby perennial for permanent landscape use. Where it would winterkill outdoors, grow it in containers and bring plants inside during the cold months.

There are several varieties of *Rosmarinus officinalis* that grow between 2 and 6 feet high (depending on variety) and can be used for ground covers and hedges (pages 24-29). The leaves of all varieties are narrow and needle-like (similar to pine needles) and are glossy green on the top and a lighter, gray-green underneath. Their aroma is resinous and pine-like. Small clusters of light lavender-blue flowers ½-inch wide cover the foliage in summer and spring, although you nearly always will find a few flowers throughout the rest of the year. With age, the stems become woody and gnarled, giving plants a rugged appearance.

The variety 'Prostratus' is the lowest growing—to about 2 feet—and makes an excellent ground cover or low hedge. Its branches twist and curve and will gracefully spill over a wall or creep around rocks. Rigid, upright branches and darker blue flowers are typical of 'Tuscan Blue'. The varieties 'Collingwood Ingram' and 'Lockwood de Forest' both have bluer flowers than the species and are lower growing.

Rosemary has several associations with the Virgin Mary. The flowers are said to have received their color when she placed her sky blue cloak over a rosemary bush to dry after washing it. It is also thought that she sought cover behind a bush of rosemary while fleeing to Egypt. Boughs of rosemary have had many uses in the past. They were carried at weddings and placed on coffins at funerals. Because the fragrance was thought to be disinfectant, rosemary branches were strewn on the floors of prisons and courts of justice to counteract the diseases that prisoners carried. The ancient Greeks and Romans burned the leaves as incense. Rosemary also was used to prevent balding and to condition hair. The leaves were sometimes placed under pillows to prevent nightmares. Rosemary is also the herb of memory, and the leaves were supposed to quicken the mind and prevent forgetfulness.

Rosemary will endure poor soil, as long as it is well drained, and hot sun. Except in very hot climates, it requires little water once it is established. It responds well to container culture and can be grown indoors.

Use the leaves fresh or dried with chicken, meats (especially lamb), stews, and vegetables. A tea can also be brewed from them. Use a branch of rosemary as a brush for applying barbecue sauce to chicken and burn sprigs in the coals just before the chicken is done—the smoke will impart rosemary's characteristic flavor to the meat.

ROSE (*Rosa* species)

Plant: shrub, hardy to 10°
  (except *R. rugosa*, to 30°)

Height: to 6 feet

Soil: moderately rich, moist

Exposure: sun

Propagation: cuttings

Uses: fragrance

Roses are perhaps the best loved and most widely planted shrub in temperate parts of the world. For an herb garden the most frequently planted ones are the old roses—particularly damask, cabbage, and sweet briar.

Cabbage rose (*R. centifolia*) has prickly stems growing to 6 feet. Pink to purple, very fragrant double flowers bloom in the late spring and early summer. *R. c. muscosa* or moss rose has flower stalks and bases covered with hairy green "moss." The flowers are mostly double, and pink, white, or red in color, and have an intense old rose fragrance.

R. damascena, the old-world damask rose, grows to 6 feet and has pale green foliage. Double blossoms appear in large clusters and are very fragrant. Colors range from pure white to red. The species flowers only in spring, but some of its varieties will blossom repeatedly through summer and fall. The variety called Kazanlik (*R. d. trigintipetala*) is grown in vast quantities in southeast Europe for its flower petals which produce attar of roses.

R. eglanteria or sweet briar is a vigorous climber to 8-12 feet. The stems are prickly and covered with dark green fragrant leaves that smell like apples. The single flowers (1½ inches across) appear singly or in clusters in the late spring, followed by reddish orange fruit. Plant 3-4 feet apart for a hedge and prune once each year in the spring.

R. gallica (French rose or "Apothecary's Rose") has 3-4 foot tall stems growing from creeping rootstocks. The leaves are smooth and dark green. The flowers have an old-rose fragrance and are about 2½ inches across. They are pink through slate blue and purple, often mottled.

R. rugosa, Ramamas rose or Sea tomato is a vigorous hardy shrub growing to 3-8 feet tall. The leaves are bright, glossy green and have distinctive heavy veins which give them a crinkled appearance. Flowers are 2-4 inches across and are single or double and pure white through pink and deep purplish red. The bright red fruit is an inch or more across, shaped like small tomatoes and very showy against the foliage. They are edible but seedy.

Since ancient Grecian times, roses have been a symbol of beauty, love, fidelity, and happiness. They are most valued for their fragrance. In the later Roman period the flower petals were strewn on the floors of banquet halls and on the streets during parades and processions. Rose water is said to have flowed from fountains, and the wealthiest classes bathed in rose wine and rose water. Cakes and other delicacies were made from the petals and fruit.

There are two myths which attribute roses to gods. One says that they came from the blood of Adonis, the other that they got their red color from the blood of Aphrodite.

Varieties of the French rose (*R. gallica*) were symbols of the two royal houses of York and Lancaster: a white flowered one for York and red for Lancaster. Their dynastic struggle against one another during the 15th century was known as the "War of the Roses" after these symbols.

Medicinally, the damask rose was used to make a syrup taken for colds and coughs.

Roses are usually grown from plants purchased from a nursery or from a mail-order rose specialist. Choose species that are suitable for your climate, as their hardiness varies. Many of the old roses will grow easily from cuttings taken at the time you prune the plants before they leaf out.

In cool-summer areas choose varieties that do not have an unusually large number of petals as they will not always open well. Pastel colors are best; dark, rich colors often tend to get "muddy." Plant in open areas to assure good air circulation, and water deeply to encourage deep root growth.

In hot-summer areas roses grow fast and strong but if planted in the hot sun they sometimes open prematurely, burn, or fade. Provide midday or afternoon shade for best summer flowers. Avoid reflected heat from light colored walls and avoid south or west exposure. Mulch heavily to conserve moisture and keep roots cool.

In cold-winter areas, select hardy plants. Plant them with bud onion just below the soil surface. After planting, mound soil over canes for protection against freezing. Begin removing soil gradually when hard freezes are over. Cut out dead branch tips in the spring.

Most roses like a well-aerated, moderately rich soil and need good watering. Feed regularly in coordination with the blooming periods—just after one period has ended and new growth is beginning for the next one is a good time. Roses are subject to aphids, spider mites, and thrips, depending on the variety and your geographic location. Spray against them as needed.

The most common use for roses is in the landscape, but you also can use the petals and fruit to make tea, jellies, potpourri, and sachets.

RUE (*Ruta graveolens*)

Plant: perennial, hardy to —20°

Height: 2-3 feet

Soil: slightly alkaline

Exposure: sun

Propagation: seeds, division

Uses: landscape only

Rue, or Herb-of-Grace, has blue-green leaves that are deeply notched and divided. Rather than ending in points however, the divisions become wider at their outer ends. Small yellow-green flowers grow several together in terminal clusters, and later turn into decorative brown seed capsules that have a beautiful carved appearance. Rue is perennial, and the stems branch upwards from the root to about 2-3 feet. The foliage has a strong, pungent aroma. The variety 'Blue Mound' has decorative blue-gray foliage.

Rue has been used in the past for medicinal purposes. King Mithridates of Pontus is said to have taken small daily doses of a mixture of rue and other poisonous herbs to make himself immune to the poisons he feared his rivals were trying to use to assassinate him. Other beliefs were that if the tip of an arrow was dipped in juice extracted from rue it would never miss its target, and that if the flints of old-fashioned guns were boiled with rue leaves, the weapon would always be accurate. The word rue means sorrow or pity, and the leaves were at one time supposed to have been added to holy water used to bless sinners in Holy Communion.

Plant rue in full sun in good, slightly alkaline garden soil. Grow new plants from seeds or divisions.

Rue is not used very much today as a culinary herb, but the seed heads are often used in arrangements, wreaths, and other dried decorations. Some persons are allergic to rue which may cause a skin rash.

SAGE (*Salvia* species)

Plant: perennial, hardy to —30°
(*S. gracilistyla* hardy to 20°)

Height: 2-3 feet

Soil: dry, well drained

Exposure: sun

Propagation: seeds, cuttings

Uses: culinary

The most familiar species is the 2-foot-tall shrubby perennial *Salvia officinalis* or garden sage. Its gray-green leaves are shaped like elongated ovals—1-2 inches long—and have a coarse surface covered with small bumps. The flowers appear on tall spikes and are usually violet-blue. The variety 'Tricolor' has leaves variegated with white and purple-red; 'Golden sage' has yellow variations on the edges of the leaves; and purple sage has deep reddish purple foliage.

Two other familiar herb garden species are pineapple sage (*S. gracilistyla*) and clary sage (*S. sclarea*). Pineapple sage is a 2-3 foot tender perennial with deliciously fragrant light green leaves and scarlet flowers in the fall. Clary sage—often grown for its pretty flowers—is biennial and has large, 6-7-inch leaves that become smaller as they approach the ends of the stems. It is the tallest of the three species and reaches 3-4 feet.

Garden sage was highly valued for its medicinal qualities and was said to cure ailments ranging from broken bones and wounds to stomach disorders and loss of memory. It was said of this herb, "How can a man die with sage growing in his garden?"

Clary sage was thought to cure eye infections and cataracts and was called "clear eye" after the custom of naming plants according to the parts of the body they were supposed to cure. The leaves of clary sage were also fried in batter, like fritters, and eaten with lamb.

Sages have been used in making beer and ale, as mouth washes and tooth cleansers, and to stimulate hair growth. Pork and roast goose were not considered well cooked unless sage had been used in preparing them.

Sage likes poor but well drained soil and full sun. It is fairly drought resistant. Over watering—especially from the top—may cause serious mildew problems. Cut back the stems after blooming. If you cut frequently for the leaves, fertilize plants occasionally with a well balanced fertilizer. You can grow new plants of all three species from seeds, and garden and pineapple sages from layers and stem cuttings; renew plants every 3 or 4 years.

Use the fresh or dried leaves with lamb, meat stuffings, sausage, cheese, and roast goose.

SANTOLINA (*Santolina* species)

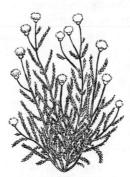

Plant: perennial, hardy to 5°

Height: 2 feet

Soil: average, well drained

Exposure: sun

Propagation: cuttings

Uses: landscape only

Both of the two common santolina species are grown for their fine appearance in the garden rather than for any culinary, medicinal, or fragrance association. Their value is as ground covers, bank covers, and low clipped hedges.

Lavender cotton (*S. chamaecyparissus*) has brittle, woody stems that may build up to 2 feet high and spread widely, rooting as they touch the soil. The narrow, rough, and finely divided leaves are whitish gray and give the mounding plants a fluffy—almost cottony—appearance. On unclipped plants, bright yellow, buttonlike flower heads appear in summertime.

S. virens is similar in all ways and uses to lavender cotton except for foliage and flower color. Its leaves are narrower and dark green, while the flower heads are a creamy chartreuse. It also is faster growing and tolerant of more watering.

The santolinas were relative latecomers to European herb gardens, missing the age of the herbalists and their imaginative plant uses. Introduced from southern Europe and Mediterranean Africa, santolinas were still not commonly grown at the time this country was settled.

The plants of both species thrive in full sun and in any garden soil that provides good drainage. Space them about 3 feet apart for ground covers, closer for hedges.

SAVORY (*Satureja* species)

Plant: annual and perennial
(*S. montana* hardy to 10°)

Height: 18 inches

Soil: light, well drained

Exposure: sun

Propagation: seeds, cuttings

Uses: culinary

There are two savories commonly grown and used as food seasonings. Summer savory (*S. hortensis*) is an annual, and the stems grow upright to about 18 inches in a loose, open fashion—often branching like a tree at maturity. Narrow, aromatic ½-1½-inch-long leaves grow in pairs along the stems, tiny flowers are a delicate pinkish white to rose color.

Winter savory (*S. montana*) is perennial and has a lower, more spreading growth form than the annual species. The stems grow to about 6-15 inches high, and are light green at the upper ends but become brown and woody at the base. Stiff, narrow to roundish leaves that are ½-1 inch long grow opposite one another in pairs, each pair being at right angles to the one below it. A profusion of ⅜-inch, white to lilac blossoms are attractive to bees.

Another species of savory is yerba buena (*S. douglasii*), the herb after which San Francisco was originally named. It is a low, creeping perennial, native to the Pacific coastal states and British Columbia. The slender stems spread to about 3 feet, rooting as they grow. The roundish, 1-inch-long leaves have scalloped edges and a strong, minty aroma. Small, white or lavender tinted flowers bloom from April to September.

Summer and winter savories are native to Southern Europe and the Mediterranean areas. The ancient Greeks called the plants *isope*, and there has been question whether savory was actually the herb meant in Old Testament references to hyssop. Savory came to England with the Norman conquest. It was used in sausages and stews and with beans, fish, and meats such as rabbit and chicken. The herbalists said that the stems and leaves could be rubbed on a bee sting to relieve the pain and itching.

Summer savory is best grown in light soil, rich with humus, and in full sun. It also makes an excellent container plant. Sow seeds where they are to grow and thin seedlings to about 18 inches apart.

Winter savory prefers sandy, well drained soil and average moisture. The stems should be kept clipped from the start of the flowering period. Because its seeds are slow to germinate, it is more satisfactory to propagate from cuttings or divisions. Winter savory is a good edging for an herb garden or border and is often grown to attract bees.

Yerba buena needs summer drought for long life if it is grown on the coast, partial shade in inland areas.

Savory leaves have a pleasant peppery flavor; that of summer savory is more delicate than the winter species and the more frequently used as a seasoning. Use the leaves fresh or dried with meats, fish, eggs, beans, and in soups. They also can be used to flavor vinegar and salad dressings. The leaves of yerba buena can be brewed into a pleasant tea.

SORREL (*Rumex* species)

Plant: perennial, hardy to —30°

Height: 2-3 feet

Soil: rich

Exposure: sun

Propagation: seeds, division

Uses: culinary

There are two common species of sorrel: garden sorrel (*R. acetosa*) and French sorrel (*R. scutatus*); both are perennial. French sorrel has large heart-shaped leaves and grows to about 2 feet. Garden sorrel is about 3 feet high, and the leaves are shaped like arrowheads.

Sorrel was once eaten as a vegetable, prepared in the same fashion spinach is today and as a green in salads. The juice of the leaves was also used to remove stains from hands.

Grow garden sorrel in a rich, moist soil and full sun. French sorrel prefers a drier soil. Both can be raised from seed and propagated by division.

The leaves of French sorrel are used to make sorrel soup and small quantities may be included in salads. They also can be cooked with spinach or cabbage. Add a fresh leaf of French sorrel to any cream soup during the last few minutes of cooking for a unique flavor. The flowers are sometimes dried and useful in dried arrangements.

SOUTHERNWOOD (*Artemisia abrotanum*)

Plant: perennial, hardy to —10°

Height: 3-5 feet

Soil: dry

Exposure: sun

Propagation: division

Uses: landscape only

This herb is a 3-5-foot woody shrub with beautiful, feathery, green foliage that has a pleasant lemon scent. The flower heads are yellowish white.

Southernwood is an ancient medicinal herb that dates back to early Rome. In the past it has been prescribed for an array of diseases and ailments, one of which was balding. Known as "lad's love" and "maiden's ruin," southernwood was once considered to be an aphrodisiac used to make a love potion. Sprigs of the foliage have been hung in closets to repel moths.

Grow southernwood in full sun and keep soil on the dry side. Divide large plants in the spring or fall.

The lemon-scented green foliage makes this herb a good shrub for perennial borders. Try burning a few leaves on the stove to kill kitchen odors.

SWEET BAY (*Laurus nobilis*)

Plant: shrub-tree, hardy to 5°

Height: up to 40 feet

Soil: average, well drained

Exposure: sun, partial shade

Propagation: nursery plants

Uses: culinary

Sweet bay or Grecian laurel is an evergreen shrub or, eventually, a tree, that grows slowly to as much as 40 feet tall in favorable locations. Its natural growth form is compact and multi-stemmed, with the foliage tapering from a broad, thick base to a cone-like point at the top. It is very attractive when clipped into formal shapes— globes, cones, and other topiary forms, standards or hedges. The dark green oval leaves are shiny and leathery, pointed at either end, and 2-4 inches long. Small, yellow flowers are followed by inch-long black or purple berries.

Though not a species of *Laurus*, California bay or Oregon myrtle (*Umbellularia californica*) has leaves that are very similar in flavor to sweet bay and can be used in the same foods.

A Mediterranean native, this is the laurel famous in ancient Greek and Roman mythology and ceremony. There is an ancient legend which gives its origin as this: Daphne was being pursued by Apollo and in distress she called to the gods to have mercy and save her. In response, the gods changed her into the laurel tree. Thereafter, the sweet bay was considered to be divine and was the favorite tree of Apollo. This is also the tree whose boughs crowned victors of war, athletic competition, and poetry contests. The term baccalaureate probably goes back to this practice—bacca meaning berry, and laureate meaning laureled; thus "covered with berries of laurel." In contrast to these celebrating associations, the withering of a laurel tree was once considered an omen of disaster.

Laurel is not particular about soil (as long as it is well drained) and requires only occasional watering once established; but it is, however, very sensitive to climate and temperature. In hot-summer regions it is best grown in filtered sun or afternoon shade. In cold areas it must be wintered indoors. Because of this it is often grown in tubs or containers which can be moved as the seasons change. Small plants should be bought from a nursery, as seeds take long to germinate and cuttings root slowly.

The fragrant leaves of laurel are almost a must in stews, spaghetti, meatloaf, and stuffings. They can be used either fresh or dried, and can be picked from an established plant at any time.

SWEET CICELY (*Myrrhis odorata*)

Plant: perennial, hardy to —20°

Height: 2-3 feet

Soil: rich, moist, well drained

Exposure: shade, partial shade

Propagation: seeds, divisions

Uses: culinary

Each lacy, delicate green leaf of sweet cicely consists of several finely-cut pairs of leaflets, so that mature plants resemble a fern or tansy. Several thin branching stems grow upright from the tap root to a height of about 2 or 3 feet. In early summer, small white flowers appear in terminal clusters about 2 inches wide. Both the seeds and leaves have a slight anise flavor. There is another plant called sweet cicely—native to woods in Western states. But, it is an entirely different plant from the sweet cicely herb and named *Osmorhiza*.

Sweet cicely has also been called sweet chervil or giant chervil by many writers. The roots were once used with wine to make a decoction taken for bites of poisonous snakes, spiders, and mad dogs.

Best growth is in shade or semi-shade. It prefers moderately rich, moist, well drained soil. The seeds take up to 8 months to germinate and are usually planted in the fall to produce seedlings the following spring. Increase your stock by dividing the roots of mature plants in the fall or early spring.

The spicy green seeds of sweet cicely can be used to give salads an anise flavor. Like fennel, the roots can be eaten raw or cooked like a vegetable.

SWEET WOODRUFF
(Asperula odorata)

Plant: perennial, hardy to —20°

Height: 6-12 inches

Soil: moist, rich

Exposure: shade

Propagation: division

Uses: tea, wine

Sweet woodruff is an attractive, low-growing perennial that will spread rapidly as a ground cover in shady areas and good moisture. The slender square stems grow 6-12 inches high, and—every inch or so—are encircled by whorls of 6-8 aromatic, bristle-tipped leaves. Clusters of tiny white flowers show above the foliage in the late spring and summer.

Along with chamomile, sweet woodruff is one of the traditional herb garden ground covers. Wreaths and garlands of the leaves and stems were hung in homes and churches where their pleasant aroma refreshed the air. In the medieval medicinal field the leaves also were placed over small cuts to stop the bleeding and to heal them.

Thrives best in moist, shady locations. You can grow this herb from small plants sold at nurseries and increase your stock by root division in the fall or spring.

The dried or crushed leaves and branches are sweet smelling like new mown hay. Use the flowers in making May Wine or steep them in boiling water for flavorful tea.

TANSY (Tanacetum vulgare)

Plant: perennial, hardy to —30°

Height: 3 feet

Soil: any soil

Exposure: sun

Propagation: seeds, division

Uses: landscape only

Tansy is a coarse, 3-foot-high perennial which dies back every year in the fall and returns the following spring. The bright green leaves are large and finely cut—like those of a large fern. Small, buttonlike yellow flowers

appear in the late summer in flat terminal clusters. A shorter variety—to 2½ feet—is *T. v. crispum,* and its foliage is more delicate, and the plant better suited as a garden ornamental than is the common species. In some parts of the western United States it has escaped from cultivation and now grows wild.

Medieval herbalists recommended this herb as a cure for a number of ills including gout, plague, colic, and cramps. A tea made from the leaves was taken in the spring and was supposed to prevent sickness during the summer. The leaves also were applied externally on the skin to remove freckles and sunburn. In cooking, it was used to flavor an egg dish known as "tansy."

Tansy will grow in almost any garden soil that is in full sun. Start it from seeds or from root divisions. Clumps of tansy should be thinned each year to keep them in bounds.

Today, tansy is not used as a seasoning, but the foliage and flowers keep well and can be used in bouquets and arrangements.

TARRAGON (Artemisia dracunculus)

Plant: perennial, hardy to —10°

Height: 1-2 feet

Soil: moderately rich, well drained

Exposure: sun, partial shade

Propagation: division, root cuttings

Uses: culinary

French tarragon is a rather prostrate, woody perennial that spreads slowly by creeping rhizomes. The shiny, dark green leaves are slender, pointed at the ends, and very aromatic. Flowers are seldom seen but are tiny and greenish white in branched clusters.

It was once believed that tarragon was the result of putting flax seeds into a cut made in the root of a radish or sea onion. The name tarragon comes from the French word *estragon* which means "little dragon," the association perhaps being with the strong flavor of the leaves.

Tarragon likes well drained, good garden soil. Plant it in a warm location and in full or partial sun. True French tarragon does not produce seeds and will have to be grown from cuttings or divisions. Propagate by root cuttings, and every 3 or 4 years you can divide established plants. This variety should not be confused with the Russian variety which looks similar except for rougher, greener leaves and which does not have the same unique flavor, although it does bear seeds.

The leaves of French tarragon have a distinctive, slightly anise-like flavor and can be used fresh or dried in salads, egg dishes, cheeses, vinegars, and with fish.

THYME (*Thymus* species)

Plant: perennial, hardy to —20°

Height: 2-12 inches

Soil: dry, light

Exposure: sun

Propagation: seeds, cuttings

Uses: culinary, ground cover

There are many species and varieties of thyme which are grown as ground covers (described on pages 24-26), for their aroma and flavor, or as ornamentals. Common thyme (*T. vulgaris*) is the species commonly used as a seasoning. It is a semi-woody, shrubby perennial that grows 6-12 inches high and can spread 1½ feet or more. Oval gray-green leaves are ¼-inch long. Small flowers grow at the ends of the stems in loose spikes. Other species of thyme are: Caraway-scented thyme (*T. herba-barona*) which forms a mat-like ground cover and has a caraway aroma; and woolly thyme (*T. lanuginosus*), another ground cover having tiny leaves. There are a great number of varieties of mother-of-thyme (*T. serpyllum*); many are planted as a filler for small areas in the garden. Silver thyme (*T. s.* 'Argenteus') has small leaves variegated with silver; lemon thyme (*T. s. vulgaris*), is grown for its wonderfully fragrant lemon-scented foliage which is variegated with yellow.

Thyme has always been a favorite herb and historically has been associated with happiness, courage, and well-being. A tea made from the leaves was taken to prevent nightmares, and one writer in the Middle Ages described a recipe for a tea made of thyme and other common wild herbs that enabled one to see the nymphs and fairies that lived in fields and meadows.

Grow thyme in warm, light, well drained soil that is fairly dry. They will withstand some neglect. Propagate by sowing seeds in containers or in the garden or from cuttings taken early in the summer. Restrain plants as necessary by clipping back the growing tips.

Use the leaves of common thyme fresh or dried in vegetable juices, stuffings, soups, and with fish, shellfish, poultry, meats, and vegetables.

VALERIAN (*Valeriana officinalis*)

Plant: perennial, hardy to —30°

Height: 4 feet

Soil: average

Exposure: sun, partial shade

Propagation: seeds, division

Uses: landscape only

Common valerian has tall, straight stems growing to about 4 feet high and rising well above the bulk of the leaves which remain fairly close to the ground. The light green leaves grow in pairs that are further divided into 8-10 pairs of narrow leaflets. The tiny flowers are white, pink, or lavender-blue and grow in rounded clusters at the ends of the stems. It is perennial, spreading by creeping underground runners, and can become rank and invasive.

Valerian has been known as all-heal and St. George's herb. In the past it was used medicinally to treat epilepsy and other ailments associated with the heart and brain.

The common name "garden heliotrope" sometimes is attached to this plant, but true heliotrope is another plant entirely. In similar manner, another plant (*Centranthus ruber*) often goes by the name "valerian" and at one time was considered a valerian species. Both of these plants are more commonly available than *Valeriana officinalis* and still sometimes sold under their misleading names.

Set plants out in good garden soil and sun or partial shade. You can propagate new plants from seeds or divisions. Valerian is a good component of mixed herb or flower borders if it is not allowed to crowd the other plants. Use the cut flowers in fresh arrangements.

VIOLETS (*Viola* species)

Plant: perennial, hardy to —20°

Height: 6-12 inches

Soil: moist, rich

Exposure: sun to shade

Propagation: seeds, division

Uses: fragrance, landscape

There are many species of violets and pansies. The two most frequently grown in herb gardens are sweet violet (V. odorata) of which many poems and songs have been written, and Johnny-jump-up (V. tricolor), or heart's ease, an herb valued in the past as a medicine.

Sweet violets have dark green, heart-shaped leaves with pointed tips and toothed margins that grow at the ends of long leaf stalks. Colors of the fragrant flowers range from deep violet, to bluish rose, to white. Several varieties are popular: 'Royal Robe' is large with deep blue blossoms; 'Marie Louise' produces fragrant, double white and bluish lavender flowers.

Johnny-jump-ups (V. tricolor) are 6-12 inches tall, and grow in tufted clumps. The flowers are purple, blue, mauve, lavender, or yellow and resemble small pansies.

Violets have been prized for their beauty, fragrance, and medicinal qualities. They were associated with humility and constancy, and have been used in spring celebrations. Herbalists have recommended them for epilepsy, skin diseases, and low spirits. Puddings, wines, jellies, salads, and a type of fritter have been made from their leaves, which contain quantities of vitamin C and were often eaten to strengthen the body.

Violets thrive in rich, moist soil. They usually need protection from hot afternoon sun, and in the desert and other hot-summer climates they should be planted in full shade. In cool-summer climates they will grow well in full sun or sun-filtered shade. Though perennials, both species, Johnny-jump-ups in particular, usually are treated as annuals. Start from seeds or buy them in flats at nurseries; sweet violets spread by runners and can be divided to give you new plants.

Sweet violets and Johnny-jump-ups are mostly used for color in the landscape and for borders. Under spring flowering bulbs, for example, they will provide mass color as a ground cover. If you fertilize sweet violets in spring before bloom, they will give you more flowers.

There are several species of wormwood suitable for the herb garden, but the most traditional representative is A. absinthium or common wormwood with its woody stems 2-4 feet tall. The finely divided leaves are silvery gray and have a bitter taste and pungent aroma. Plants need a periodic pruning to maintain a good, compact shape. A. frigida, or fringed wormwood, grows about 1-1½ feet high and has white, finely-cut leaves. Young plants are compact, but cut them back when they start to become rangy. Roman wormwood (A. pontica) is a 4-foot shrub with silver-gray, feathery leaves and inconspicuous whitish yellow flowers.

Sagebrush (A. tridentata) is an evergreen shrub native to the Great Basin region of the West. It grows between 1½-15 feet high and has many branching stems. The narrow green leaves have a hairy surface and are about ¾-inch long. They are very aromatic.

The best known use of common wormwood was in making absinthe in which it acted as a narcotic. It is one of the bitterest herbs and was used to cure a number of diseases and to season cakes and beverages. It is now an important ingredient in Vermouth and liqueurs. There is a European folk belief that if a traveler carries a sprig of its foliage with him he will not become tired. It has also been placed among clothing to repel moths. Sagebrush was used by desert Indians in medicine, dyes, foods, and as sacred wands for medicine men.

Wormwood is drought resistant and grows best in full sun. Divide plants in the spring or fall.

Artemisias are most commonly used in the garden for their ornamental gray color, especially as a gray accent in borders of green plants or colorful flowers. The silvery-gray foliage softens harsh reds and oranges and blends beautifully with blues, lavenders, and pinks.

Use common wormwood sparingly to season poultry. Roman wormwood is sometimes added to sachets. Place leaves in closets to keep moths away.

WORMWOOD (Artemisia species)

Plant: perennial, hardy to —30°

Height: 1-4 feet

Soil: dry, poor

Exposure: sun

Propagation: cuttings, division

Uses: culinary, fragrance

YARROW (Achillea species)

Plant: perennial, hardy to —30°

Height: 8 inches to 5 feet

Soil: average, dry

Exposure: sun, partial shade

Propagation: division

Uses: landscape only

The yarrows are hardy perennials that grow in thick, bushy clumps and range in size from less than 6 inches high (ground cover species) to others that reach 5 feet. They all bear striking, flat flower clusters in white, yellows, or shades of red during the summer. The gray-green foliage has a bitter aroma when crushed.

Greek yarrow (A. ageratifolia) forms a low mat of silvery, nearly smooth-edged leaves. Clusters of white flowers are ½-1 inch wide on stems 4-10 inches tall.

Silvery yarrow (A. clavennae argentea) has loose clusters of white flowers at the tops of 5 to 10-inch stems. The leaves are silver-gray and lobed (similar to chrysanthemum leaves).

Fernleaf yarrow (A. filipendulina) has upright stems from 4 to 5 feet high, topped with 5-inch-wide clusters of chrome-yellow flowers. The deep green leaves are finely divided and fernlike. Several varieties are available: 'Gold Plate' has 6-inch-wide flower clusters; 'Coronation Gold' grows only 3 feet tall but has the same large flower clusters of 'Gold Plate'; 'Parker' grows from 2-3 feet tall and has deep golden flowers. All of these varieties make fine cut flowers for arrangements.

Common yarrow or milfoil (A. millefolium) varies from erect to spreading but all varieties may spread outward along the ground or grow erect to about 3 feet high. Flowers are white or red and the foliage varies from green to gray-green.

A. nana grows only 2-8 inches high and has white flowers in dense flat clusters. Its woolly leaves are divided into short, sharp-pointed segments. This species will spread by underground runners.

A. 'Moonshine' has bright sulfur-yellow flowers growing on 18 to 24-inch stems.

A. ptarmica is a white flowered species with narrow finely toothed, green leaves. Plants are upright to about 2 feet.

A. taygetea. The flowers of this species appear in dense clusters and are bright yellow when they first open but soon change to soft primrose yellow. The plants grow 18 inches tall with gray-green, finely divided leaves 3-4 inches long.

Woolly yarrow (A. tomentosa) forms a low spreading mat of deep green fernlike foliage and makes a good ground cover in sunny or partially shaded places. Golden colored flowers grow at the top of the 6-10-inch stems.

Common yarrow is an old medicinal herb and is supposed to have been used by Achilles to stop the bleeding of his wounded men in the Trojan Wars, and from him yarrow gained its generic name. Since then it was used to cure cuts and has been called wound wort, nosebleed, and sanguinary. In the past, a tea brewed from the leaves was taken to relieve colds.

All of the yarrows grow best in full sun and require only very moderate watering. If the plants are cut back after the first flowers fade, they'll generally bloom a second time in the fall. Plants soon form large clumps and need dividing about every other year. Yarrows are hardy in all areas.

The yarrows are most useful in the landscape where they can act as ground covers, border fillers, color, and accent. The flowers are very pretty and useful in arrangements.

Index

PHOTO CREDITS

William Aplin: back cover, page 17, 23 (top), 25 (top), 28 (bottom), 31 (bottom), 33 (top right), 46. Morley Baer: page 30 (top). Ernest Braun: page 16. Robert Cox: pages 54 and 21 (top right). Glenn M. Christiansen: page 19 (bottom right). Dick Dawson: page 19 (bottom left). Gerald R. Fredrick: page 31 (top). Alyson Smith Gonsalves: pages 7 (right), 8 (left), 10 (bottom right), 11 (all), 12, 20 (top), 26 (top left), 33 (top right), 34, 35 (all), 41 (top), 42, 43 (all), 44 (all), 45 (all), 47, 48 (bottom), 49. Art Hupy: pages 8 (right) and 15. Richard Jepperson: page 23 (bottom). Ells Marugg: front cover. Don Normark: pages 18, 19 (top), 20 (bottom), 21 (bottom), 24, 25 (bottom left), 26 (top right), 28 (top), 33 (bottom left). Marjorie Ray Piper: page 32 (bottom). Norman A. Plate: pages 25 (bottom right), 48 (top), 50 (all). Tom Riley: page 14. John Robinson: pages 27 and 29 (all). George Selland, Moss Photography: page 38. Hugh N. Stratford: pages 10 (top) and 22 (bottom). Mike Tilden: page 4. Darrow M. Watt: pages 7 (left), 9, 21 (top left), 22 (top), 30 (bottom), 32 (top), 33 (bottom right), 36, 37, 41 (bottom).